A catalogue record for this title is available from The British Library

ISBN 0 340 648368

First published 1996
Impression number 10 9 8   7 6   5 4   3 2
Year   1999 1998 1997 1996

"Good Girls Go To Heaven (Bad Girls Go Everywhere)"
Written by Jim Steinman
© 1989 PolyGram International Music Publishing B.V.
Lyrics reproduced by kind permission of the publisher

Typeset by Transet Limited, Coventry, England
Printed in Great Britain for Hodder & Stoughton Educational, a division of Hodder
Headline plc, 338 Euston Road, London NW1 3BH by Cox and Wyman Limited,
Reading.

THE MOON AND YOU
for beginners

TERESA MOOREY

Headway · Hodder & Stoughton

Other titles in this series

Chakras The body's energy centres, the chakras, can act as gateways to healing and increased self-knowledge. This book shows you how to work with chakras in safety and with confidence.

Chinese Horoscopes In the Chinese system of horoscopes, the *year* of birth is all-important. *Chinese Horoscopes for beginners* tells you how to determine your own Chinese horoscopes, what personality traits you are likely to have, and how your fortunes may fluctuate in years to come.

Dowsing People all over the world have used dowsing since the earliest times. This book shows how to start dowsing – what to use, what to dowse, and what to expect when subtle energies are detected.

Dream Interpretation This fascinating introduction to the art of science of dream interpretation explains how to unravel the meaning behind dream images to interpret your own and other people's dreams.

Feng Shui This beginner's guide to the ancient art of luck management will show you how to increase your good fortune and well-being by harmonising your environment with the natural energies of the earth.

Gems and Crystals For centuries gems and crystals have been used as an aid to healing and meditation. This guide tells you all you need to know about choosing, keeping and using stones to increase your personal awareness and improve your well-being.

Graphology Graphology, the science of interpreting handwriting to reveal personality, is now widely accepted and used throughout the world. This introduction will enable you to make a comprehensive analysis of your own and other people's handwriting to reveal the hidden self.

I Ching The roots of *I Ching* or *The Book of Changes* lie in the time of the feudal mandarin lords of China, but its traditional wisdom is still relevant today. Using the original poetry in its translated form, this introduction traces its history, survival and modern day applications.

Love Signs This is a practical introduction to the astrology of romantic relationships. It explains the different roles played by each of the planets, focusing particularly on the position of the Moon at the time of birth.

Meditation This beginner's guide gives simple, clear instructions to enable you to start meditating and benefiting from this ancient mental discipline immediately. The text is illustrated throughout by full-colour photographs and line drawing.

Numerology Despite being scientifically based, numerology requires no great mathematical talents to understand. This introduction gives you all the information you will need to understand the significance of numbers in your everyday life.

Palmistry Palmistry is the oldest form of character reading still in use. This illustrated guide shows you exactly what to look for and how to interpret what you find.

Runes The power of runes in healing and giving advice about relationships and life in general has been acknowledged since the time of the Vikings. This book looks shows how runes can be used in our technological age to increase personal awareness and stimulate individual growth.

Star Signs This detailed analysis looks at each of the star signs in turn and reveals how your star sign affects everything about you. This book shows you how to use this knowledge in your relationships and in everyday life.

Tarot Tarot cards have been used for many centuries. This guide gives advice on which sort to buy, where to get them and how to use them. The emphasis is on using the cards positively, as a tool gaining self-knowledge, while exploring present and future possibilities.

Visualisation This introduction to visualisation, a form of self-hypnosis widely used by Buddhists, will show you how to practise the basic techniques – to relieve stress, improve your health and increase your sense of personal well-being.

CONTENTS

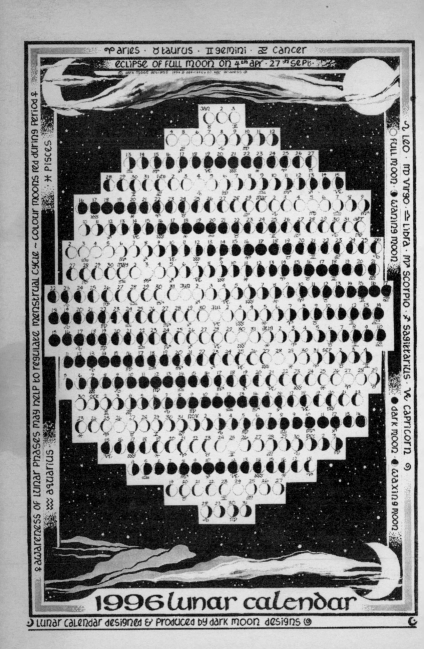

1996 lunar calendar

Lunar calendar designed & produced by dark moon designs

INTRODUCTION

Hey, Janey, Janey, why are you crying?
There's a beauty of a moon in the sky.
But I guess when you've been leading such a sheltered life
You never lift your head and look so high

Good Girls Go to Heaven (Bad Girls Go Everywhere)
Meat Loaf (Writer Jim Steinman)

Do you know the phase of the Moon at the present moment? Did you notice her in the sky last night? If so, how did you feel? In our time of street lamps and neon signs we are apt to forget about the Moon – but she is important, and she has been since time began. Watched and worshipped, she has smiled on lovers and has inspired poets. As our nearest neighbour in space she has challenged scientists, and the struggle to reach her has produced many discoveries. However, she seems to have proved uninteresting – she is not made of cheese and there is no 'man' in her. Indeed she is barren and airless. Her seas are deserts of dust. She has been de-mystified.

But has she? Isn't moonlight just as enchanting as ever? The fact is that for us on earth the Moon *is* magical. We need a sense of meaning as well as facts. Our scientific approach is only one way; it is not the only way. Science has given us many wonderful things but it has also left us high and dry. Our Newtonian idea of a clockwork universe is ironical, for Newton himself was a mystic, and a student of astrology. When challenged on this by the astronomer Halley (of comet fame) he is reported to have said 'I have studied it, Sir, you have not'. None the less we have largely inherited a universe without a soul.

1

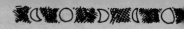

Science is slowly coming round. Chaos theory and quantum physics are beginning to reveal fresh perspectives. However, the majority of us whose ways of thinking lag behind Einstein have to rely on intuition and inner conviction to reveal other aspects of reality. The wonder of existence can't be put into a formula. A part of us knows that the Moon is more than a mere lump of rock.

This book is about the importance of the Moon, in several ways. We shall be looking briefly at some of what she symbolises, what her phases are and how we can 'tune in' to them to help us feel more 'whole'. We will also examine the meaning of the phase under which we were born, and how we can use this knowledge to become more effectual and harmonious. To find your birth phase, consult the tables on pages 144 and 145.

Of course, we are all much more than our Moon phase or Sun sign, and if you are serious about knowing yourself through astrology you will need to have your whole chart drawn up by an astrologer (see page 150). Meanwhile, maybe this book can begin to arouse your interest and increase your awareness of the Moon and all that she means.

A Note on Relaxation

Each Moon-phase section in the book includes a visualisation exercise. Before doing this it is advisable to make yourself comfortable and relax totally, preferably on your bed. You may like to do this by tensing each muscle in turn and then relaxing it. Start at your toes and work upwards until you have reached the top of your head. Then check through once more to be sure no tension has crept back.

Or you may prefer to imagine you are a candle with a flame at your head. The hot wax is rolling softly down over you, taking away all the tension and worries with it.

If you are not used to relaxing consciously in this way it may take you several weeks to perfect. Set aside a time each day when you can practise – ten minutes a day is better than an hour once a week.

If you like, you can record the exercise on tape – if you don't like your own voice, get a friend to do it for you. Don't worry if you are one of those people who cannot visualise. Maybe you will hear, smell or feel things instead. In any case, allow yourself to feel warm and comfortable. The words will take effect anyway. Remember to make the affirmations, as directed. Take these short visualisations very slowly – relaxing plus visualising should take 15 minutes, at least.

It does not matter if you fall asleep – it shows you needed the rest. If you have commitments, set an alarm clock. Take note of any dreams you have. If the falling asleep becomes a habit you may prefer to do the exercises sitting up, in a suitable chair. Feel free to expand the visualisations, or let yourself explore them further while in your relaxed state. Always give yourself time to 'come round' at the end. Eat or drink a little something. If you regularly feel depleted after the exercises say to yourself, before you start, 'While relaxed I am safe and protected. There is a sphere of light around me keeping away all harm.' Visualise a shimmering blue sphere around you, if you can. Alternatively you may like to say a short prayer.

MOON PHASE AND GODDESS

Behold the Three-Formed Goddess
She who is ever Three – Maid, Mother and Crone;
Yet is she ever One.

Prayer to the Goddess

WOMEN AND THE GODDESS IN HISTORY

Thousands of years ago people worshipped a Great Mother who gave birth to all life. There are numerous prehistoric monuments that show this and many apparently pregnant goddess figurines, have been discovered. One example is the 'Venus of Willendorf', dating from 30,000 BC.

The Celts believed that only by re-entering the womb of the Mother could a man enter the blessed Land of the Dead, Tir-na-nog. Femaleness was valued for its own sake, not as a result of a struggle for equality, and it seems that society was generally matrilinear (which means that the blood-line was passed down from mother to daughter, not from father to son). As shamans – magical priests – and tribal leaders, women would have held considerable power. Of course there is much about these times that we would not wish to return to, even if we could. None the less, feeling is growing that ancient peoples possessed much basic wisdom that we have lost.

While early 'nature worshippers' saw the Earth as the body of the

Goddess, links with the Moon were also noticed. Women menstruate, and this more or less monthly rhythm often corresponds to the Moon's phases. The Moon's cycle was used for measurement – hence such words as *menstruation*, *mensuration*, *month*, *commensurate* and *dimension*. The circle at Stonehenge is held to be a megalithic computer, designed in part to calculate phases and eclipses.

Ways of measurement came from the Moon because she seemed to measure what people then recognised as important – the forces of life. We use the Sun to measure the years and days of our conscious actions, but the Moon is the 'clock of our instincts'. It is easy to dismiss all of this, and hard to put its importance into words, for words are the tool of the conscious mind, except when used in poetry. However, many people are all too aware that something has been lost. Feelings of depression, and pointlessness are common. The Moon can show us one way to feel connected and joyful, if we listen to her rhythms.

The three phases

The three phases of the Moon also seemed to correspond to the three stages in the life of an adult woman: Maiden, Mother and Crone. Hence the Triple Goddess, ever-changing yet ever-constant, Goddess of life, love, death, birth and rebirth, ruling all of creation from womb to tomb. The Moon was – and is – her shining embodiment.

The Moon's waxing phase spans about nine and a half days, from New Moon until she is bright in the sky. This is the Maiden time. The Maiden is Goddess of inspiration. She brings energy, enterprise and new beginnings. Bright, adventurous and untamed, she is free and vibrant with potential. Traditionally her colour is white.

The Full phase occupies the following nine and a half days. This is the time of the Mother. She gives birth to projects, ideas and creations of all sorts. She nurtures and brings to fulfilment. She makes things blossom and bear fruit. She brings rich gifts and

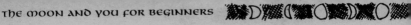

celebration. She blesses our projects and shows us what is not viable, so that we may begin again. Her traditional colour is red.

The waning phase is the final nine and a half days of the cycle, as the Moon appears later and later, thinner and thinner in the night sky, until she finally disappears. This is the time of the Crone, Goddess of Wisdom. She rules the hidden, the mysterious, the incommunicable. She shows us the need to analyse, reflect, withdraw – and perhaps to destroy so that we may eventually be able to build anew. To some she has sounded fearsome, but she is Goddess of peace and rest. The Crone shows us the need to make time for quiet in our lives. Her traditional colour is black.

We need to mention here that the Phase Cycle –i.e. the Moon's passage from New to New again – takes 29½ days, not 28 days as some people assume. However, it does take the Moon nearly 28 days to move around the zodiac – that is from the beginning of Aries all the way round through the other signs and back to the start of Aries again. Let us call this the Zodiac Cycle. This is the journey that the Sun takes a year to complete. This is quite distinct from the Phase Cycle.

Phases depend on the astronomical relationship between Earth, Sun and Moon, which we shall be looking at in Chapter 2. It is also often said that there are 13 lunar months in the year (as opposed to calendar months). As 13 x 28 = 364, that is about right for the Zodiac Cycle, but that doesn't mean there are 13 Full and New Moons each year, for these depend on Phase Cycle. Remember, the Phase Cycle takes 29½ days and 29½ x 13 = 383½. As there are only 365 days in the year it simply does not fit in. Most years have 13 New Moons or 13 Full Moons, but never both – and some years just miss out and only have 12 of each.

The dark of the Moon

Returning to our look at the Goddess, we need to mention that she has also been given a fourth aspect, an impenetrable side that has been linked to the 'dark of the Moon' – that three- or four-day

period when the Moon is not visible at all (whatever the weather!) when she is moving from Old to New. This is the Goddess 'present and unseen'. We can think about this and use our imaginations or meditate in order to draw closer to hidden parts of ourselves. Like the Triple Goddess, she lives in all of us and is personal to each. If the Crone stands at the gateway to the mysteries, this Goddess is the Mystery itself. She is not part of the Trilogy, and yet she is part of each: Maiden, Mother and Crone. This has no place in the birth phase cycle, because it is a very mystical aspect. Therefore the cycle has been divided between the three other aspects. However, the 'hidden' face must not be forgotten.

The Moon's gender

Because of the Moon's cyclical nature she seems essentially feminine, but there are many cultures where she has been seen as masculine – notably the Eskimo and the Japanese. Also it was believed – for example by the Maoris – that it was the Moon that impregnated women. The early Celts, a strongly matrifocal society, saw both Sun and Moon as feminine. Myths have many meanings and contain apparent contradictions, reminding us that existence is anything but simple.

Of course the Triple Goddess has a male counterpart, often called the Horned God. He is joyful and caring. He is described in another title in this series, *Paganism for Beginners*.

Each woman can be seen as having an inner masculine quality, called her *animus*. This 'inner man' is a source of energy and support – but also sometimes confusion. The same is true for men, who have an inner woman or *anima*. While observing the Moon and her rhythms can strengthen a woman's sense of her femininity, it can equally strengthen a man's connection with his anima, and so serve to deepen his sensitivity and creativity. We shall be looking at some simple ways of acknowledging the Moon later on, but there are no complex rituals: we just need an attitude of openness.

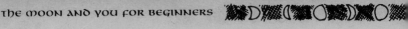

The Triple Goddess

One of the oldest forms of the Goddess is the Triple Goddess, but there have been many goddess-forms throughout history. Most goddesses are in a way linked to the Moon, but there have been some specific ones. Selene was the Greek Moon goddess, poignantly in love with Endymion, who had been granted immortality on condition that he remained asleep. So Selene looked down on him with love and longing each night. Luna was the Roman Moon goddess, hence such words as *lunar*, *lunatic* and *lunation* (meaning the Moon's phases). The Inca Moon goddess was called Mama Quilla, married to the Sun god Inti, who was her co-ruler. Levanah was the Chaldean (Babylonian) Moon goddess, called Lebanah in the 'Song of Solomon'.

There are many groups of three goddesses, such as the Norns of Teutonic mythology, who correspond to the Greek 'Fates'. There are also the Three Graces, and the Furies. Sometimes there is a three-times-three grouping of nine, such as the Nine Muses. The symbolism behind this is that all of the three aspects of the Goddess are present in each. In the end all goddesses are one Goddess. They simply embody her different aspects.

Goddesses have also been linked to specific phases. For instance, Artemis, the Maiden Huntress, is one of the goddesses of the waxing Moon. Brigit, goddess of fertility, inspiration and poetry, has been linked to all three phases, and Egyptian Isis, daughter of Earth and Sky – one of the most 'complete' goddess-forms in history – is also associated with the Full Moon.

More sinister figures are Kali (goddess of apparent destruction, but also feminine independence), Hecate (of the Underworld and magic), and Tiamat (dragon-goddess of the primordial sea). These are associated with the Moon as she wanes (although Hecate and Kali, especially, can also be linked to the 'dark of the Moon'). They are only frightening when we do not understand the message in their stories, which can help to show us the fruitfulness of darkness and the things we associate with it.

Femininity

What we are looking at is important because it gives a place to the specifically feminine in our ideas about deity. This may be unfamiliar, but it is worth considering. It is hard for the idea of a sole masculine, law-giving God to give true importance to the feminine, instinctual side of us, the side that would care for our habitat as a matter of course. An invisible God 'up in heaven', leaves the world of matter empty and unimportant – something to be overcome or exploited. So we have a runaway science that has become a kind of god itself, and we have nuclear arms, deforestation and pollution – all the tired old things that we are so used to hearing about that we despair, or simply 'tune out'.

This can also imply that women have less to offer than men. Of course very few people would seriously imply that women are inferior. However, the words 'matter' and 'mother' are related in meaning, and in our history the material world has tended to be exploited, reviled or disregarded. Women are connected to their bodies in a way that men are not because of all the biological necessities of childbirth. To be regarded as equal to men, women often feel they have to become hard-headed and ambitious, while men still strive to conceal their emotions. Despite all the new thinking, such attitudes die hard. Perhaps because of this an idea of a 'goddess' is important, because it can give extra life to developing beliefs of the 'New Age'. The Goddess is not merely an abstract: she is 'the beauty of the green earth and the white moon among the stars' (from a traditional Goddess invocation called 'The Charge', gracefully revised by Doreen Valiente). Of course the Goddess isn't just the Earth, or the Moon or anything else, but they are part of her and they symbolise her.

We know that the Earth is not flat, or the centre of the universe, or even very important in the solar system. However, we are creatures of earth, and we take our bearings from this position, for it is important to us. From our standpoint on earth the Moon can tell us a lot about the Goddess, about our instinctual natures and how to connect with them. She has a place in fulfilling the 'Goddess-shaped

9

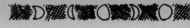

yearning' of mankind, that the author Geoffrey Ashe speaks of. This is as important to men as to women, for the men suffer, too, if the 'feminine' is devalued, but in different ways.

By observing the Moon and her rhythms we can more readily connect with Earth, and with our own bodies, which are after all largely composed of water, and so perhaps sensitive to the Moon as the tides are. We can also connect with our inner rhythms that have been repressed by the routine of work. We can get to know ourselves better and, if we are lucky, glimpse something that will fill us with wonder and a sense of meaning. There is nothing very esoteric about this. Really it's just a matter of opening up, tuning in, drawing back the curtains and letting the Moon shine in.

PRACTICE

From the above it is clear that the three stages of the Moon's cycle lend themselves to different sorts of activity. Perhaps you would like to think about how this affects you. For instance, perhaps you will feel comfortable if you start things off when the Moon is waxing (Maiden). This is a great time for all new ideas. They seem to spring into action.

Full Moon (Mother) is a good time to 'pull things together'. Many people feel full of energy at this time. Things fall into place, efforts bear fruit and many things seem clearer. Sometimes it now becomes very easy to see what is not going to work. This is a good time to bring projects to culmination. It's also a brilliant time for a party.

When the Moon is waning (Crone) may be a good time to take more rest – the more so the closer to New Moon we get. Think about the meaning of your projects, analyse, get rid of some things. It's a good time for culling that which is unnecessary in our lives, and for meditation.

Of course no one can, or should, be ruled by the Moon's phases. You're looking for harmony, smoothness – not a set of regulations. Circumstances will often oblige us to do something at a phase of the Moon that is not ideal. However, Moon phase is worth bearing

Note the Moon's phases in your calendar or diary. Make a point of looking for her in the sky. Go for walks in the moonlight. Begin to notice fluctuations in your emotions, energy levels and ways of thinking that are linked to the phases. Think about the different goddess-aspects at the appropriate phases. Do they mean anything to you? If so, what? You may like to make notes about what occurs to you in a diary or special notebook.

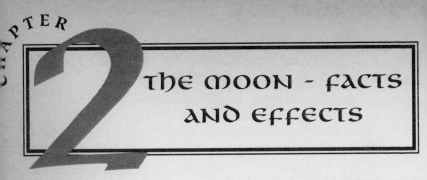

2 THE MOON - FACTS AND EFFECTS

Nothing exists or happens in the visible sky that is not sensed in some hidden manner by ... Earth and Nature.

Johannes Kepler, *De Stella Nova*

ASTRONOMY, ASTROLOGY AND SYNCHRONICITY

Astronomers investigate the heavenly bodies, and so astronomy is a science. Astrologers on the other hand interpret what the stars and planets mean for us on earth. This has been called both a science and an art, and really involves both. The early observers were both astrologers and astronomers, and it was the search for meanings that gave rise to exploration. Few astrologers believe that the planets 'make us' do things, any more than our actions influence the planets. However, the movements of Sun, Moon and planets are 'synchronous' with events on earth. In other words they are connected by something other than cause and effect. A strange thought? Maybe, but it is the only explanation for many phenomena. C. G. Jung, one of the greatest intellects of our time, set this out in his book *Synchronicity* – an important-sounding word for something that has been with us since the beginning of time.

As our nearest neighbour in space, the Moon's effects are the easiest to observe. Some are easily explainable, like the movement of the tides caused by the Moon's gravity; others are more mysterious, but

are none the less supported by statistics and observation. It is easy to see the cause of some of the Moon's effects, but others are more 'synchronous'.

An astrologer can interpret character from a chart of the heavens, drawn up for the place and time of birth. Most people know where the Sun is in their chart. For instance, if you are an Aries, that means that the Sun, seen from an earth perspective was in the part of the Zodiac we call Aries when you were born. The Sun is the conscious, decision-making part of us and most of us are well aware that we are like our Sun sign. The Moon on the other hand represents our instincts and responses, and we may be less familiar with this, although it is just as important. All the other planets also have meanings – for instance Mars means assertion, but these don't concern us here. Among other things astrologers interpret the Sun, Moon and planets according to their position in the zodiac. However, in the case of the Moon, phase is also important.

The phases

Phases have nothing to do with the zodiac, but depend on the relationship between Earth, Sun and Moon. As the Moon grows from New to Full, and then shrinks and becomes older and older until she is born again at the next New Moon, an energy tide can be felt, flowing and ebbing, affecting all of life on Earth. So the phase of the Moon when we were born affects our character and our life. The three stages, Waxing, Full and Waning, divide again into three, corresponding to nine stages in the cycle of the Moon. and so there are nine personality types depending on the Moon's phase at our birth.

The diagram on page 14 shows the phases of the Moon and what they look like at the birth time of the types.

The Moon is called 'waxing' when she is growing from New to Full, and after Full Moon up until the following New Moon she is called 'waning'. As seen from Earth, when the Moon is waxing, her 'horns'

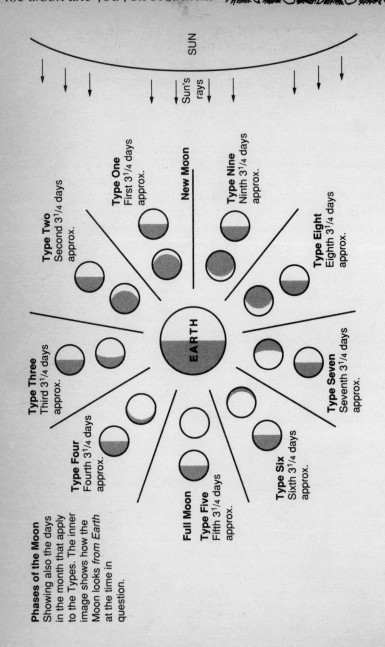

SUN

Sun's rays

Type Two
Second 3¹/4 days approx.

Type One
First 3¹/4 days approx.

New Moon

Type Nine
Ninth 3¹/4 days approx.

Type Three
Third 3¹/4 days approx.

Type Eight
Eighth 3¹/4 days approx.

EARTH

Type Four
Fourth 3¹/4 days approx.

Type Seven
Seventh 3¹/4 days approx.

Full Moon
Type Five
Fifth 3¹/4 days approx.

Type Six
Sixth 3¹/4 days approx.

Phases of the Moon
Showing also the days in the month that apply to the Types. The inner image shows how the Moon looks *from Earth* at the time in question.

14

point to the left – if we raise our right hand, curving the palm, we can seem to 'cup' the waxing Moon. Do this with the left for the waning Moon, unless you are in the Southern Hemisphere, where the reverse applies. The waxing Moon can be seen in the early evening, the waning Moon appears in the small hours. The Full Moon rides high at midnight, and for the few days just before and just after New Moon the Moon is invisible.

Although it appears that the Sun, Moon and Earth are 'in line' at New and Full (see diagram 1) this is usually not quite exact. When it is exact an eclipse occurs. Eclipses of the Sun occur at New Moon, when the Moon obscures the Sun. Eclipses of the Moon occur at Full Moon, when the Earth passes between Sun and Moon.

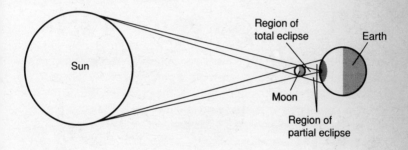

Eclipse of the Sun

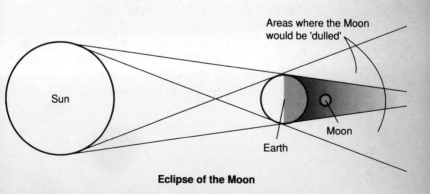

Eclipse of the Moon

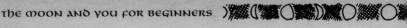

Both sorts of eclipses were frightening to ancient peoples, who thought they foretold disaster and the death of the ruler. You may like to look up the times of eclipses in your diary, or in an ephemeris – a book giving planetary positions. Solar eclipses have rather a stifling effect, sometimes creating a feeling of lethargy and pointlessness. Lunar ones can seem numbing for a while, dulling the sparkle and imagination. However, these are highly charged times and in retrospect one can often see they marked the start or end of something. If an eclipse falls on a significant point of your natal chart it will have special importance for you, but in order to know whether this is the case you will need an astrologer to draw up your chart (see 'Useful Addresses' at the end of the book). Eclipses have much influence that we do not have the space to investigate here.

SOME ASTRONOMICAL FACTS

The Moon is 238, 840 miles away, her diameter measures just over a quarter of the Earth's and her surface gravity is 0.165 that of Earth. She has only a fiftieth of the volume of Earth. The Moon has little or no atmosphere, and she is dry – her 'seas' are large plains of dust. Contrary to what used to be believed, it now seems unlikely that the Moon was ever part of the Earth, because of the differences between lunar and Earth rock.

The effects on Earth

Despite having landed on the Moon we are far from knowing all there is to know about her. Among those things yet to be explained are the clouds and lightning seen on the Moon, and the fact that stars sometimes seem to pass in front of the Moon, for a time, rather than behind.

Statistics apparently confirm what mankind has always sensed – namely that the phases of the Moon affect life on Earth. At the time of the Full Moon admissions to mental hospitals rise, and there is an increase in suicide, arson and violent crime. Surgery performed

at the Full Moon is more likely to result in haemorrhage, and studies have shown that seeds germinate faster and plants grow more quickly under a waxing Moon. Oysters brought inland have been observed to open and close in rhythm with the tides of their place of origin – at first. After a while, however, this changed and they opened and closed in direct response to the Moon overhead. We are at least as sensitive as oysters, although we may not always be conscious of our feelings.

The Moon has many links with human fertility. Not only do her phases correspond (more or less) to menstruation, but exposure to the light of the Moon can regulate a woman's cycle, promoting ovulation at Full Moon and stimulating the period at New Moon. Periods seem more likely to coincide with New or Full Moon than one of the quarters. Some surveys have suggested that a woman is more likely to conceive when the Moon is at the same phase as at her time of birth, and there seem to be more births around the times of the Full and New Moon. (This has been borne out to some extent by my studies.) Women who have problems conceiving may find that exposure to the light of the Full Moon helps. Pregnancy, described in the textbooks as lasting 40 weeks, is actually usually nine moons (i.e. 9 x 29½ days) from conception to birth.

The nine Types

In Chapter 1 we looked at the meaning of the three main phases of the Moon, and it isn't hard to see that this would naturally give rise to three basic sorts of personality, according to Moon phase at birth. The Waxing Moon relates to an 'innocent' type of person. This doesn't mean they're less prone to misdemeanours than the rest of us, but there is a childlike side to them: enthusiastic, outgoing – and sometimes thoughtless. They are more inclined to be simple souls, in the best sense of the word.

The Full phase relates more to an accepting personality, seeing contrasts and results. There may seem to be greater stillness about them than is found in the Waxing stage, but they can be observant,

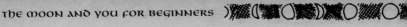

creative and very dynamic. Often they are content and like to enjoy themselves, but they may be complacent.

The Waning phase relates to those people who see meanings, values, disadvantages – who look beyond and analyse and wonder. Life often seems more complex to these folk. Sometimes they can appear more serious than the other two phases, but they can have a quirky sense of humour.

For a more exact description of personality, each of these three subdivide into another three, giving nine in all. There are sometimes groups of nine goddesses, as we have seen, meaning that each of the Three has within her the whole trio. This relates to the birth phases in that the Waxing time contains within it Waxing/Waxing (New Moon, our Type One) Waxing/Full (Type Two) and Waxing/Waning (Type Three) and so on. Nine is a number sacred to the Moon in the mystical doctrine called the Qabalah. Two and seven are numbers also linked to the Moon by tradition – and these add up to nine! I have found that the idea of nine types applies to people I have looked at. However, I do stress the dividing line between each of the types is not rigid. As the Moon swells and shrinks, so one phase develops into another.

New Moon and Full Moon have sometimes been seen as polar opposites, and this could give rise to only eight personality types. However, this does not seem to be in line with experience of the Moon's energies. Full Moon is a climax that rises, culminates and ebbs, whereas New Moon feels like a beginning. There seems to be an energy resurgence on the day of the New Moon, as if someone has turned on a light in a dark room. So the day of the New Moon corresponds to the end of Type Nine and the beginning of Type One, whereas the day of the Full Moon corresponds to the *middle* of Type Five – the Full Moon type. To get a full picture of what I mean, it is best to study the diagram on page 14. This diagram also gives an idea of how the Moon appears at your birthphase – which you can find from the tables at the back of this book.

PRACTICE

Look up the phase of the Moon when you were born in the table at the back of the book. However, don't be too literal about this. The phases of the Moon aren't marked out distinctly, like the signs of the zodiac – they blend into each other. You should also read the interpretations given for the types on either side of yours. For instance, if you come out as Type One on the table, read the interpretations for Type Nine and Type Two as well. The descriptions are to make your birth phase come alive for you, but remember if you want to know more you need your whole chart drawn up.

The Moon relates to instincts, primarily, but to see these in action we need a character-sketch. Although we often talk about 'goddess' it all applies equally to men, who also have instincts and emotions.

Astrological research

As far as I am aware very little work has been done on Moon phase, and Dane Rudhyar seems to be the only astrologer to have addressed the importance of birth phase in the natal chart. My types have characteristics in common with his, except that I divide the cycle into nine, not eight. Thus each of my types spans 40 degrees of the zodiac – although I do not think this division need be rigid, as the types blend together round the edges. Rudhyar's Full Moon type starts at full Moon, whereas I have found that the time around Full Moon, both before and after, relates to the Full Moon type – both the applying opposition to the Sun and the separating. It doesn't seem appropriate to divide the Moon cycle into an even number – perhaps that is a solar concept, unfitting for the Moon's cycle.

Needless to say, phase needs to be considered in the light of the whole chart. Also I believe the precise Sun – Moon aspect modifies phase – for instance an applying Sun – Moon trine would fall into

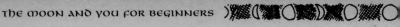

Type Three. However, it might be more appropriate to consider it as Type Four, especially if the Sun and Moon are in the same element.

Neither do the phases necessarily have to be exactly the same in length. Temporally this is not the case anyway, as the mean daily motion of the Moon is subject to variation.

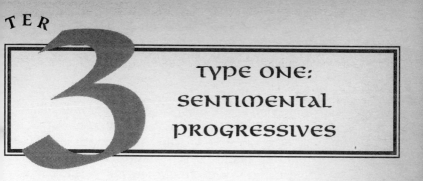

TYPE ONE: SENTIMENTAL PROGRESSIVES

Little bird on your maiden flight
Tidy goddess that sits in my palm ...
Spring flower blossoming brave and wild
Rosy angel riding with the stars.

Carolyn Hillyer, 'Little Bird' (from the album *Heron Valley*, and the book *Two Drumbeats: Songs of the Sacred Earth*, Seventh Wave Music, 1993)

Who's that whistling in the shower before anyone else is awake, at the office in time to make the tea before the sleepy-eyes roll in? It's likely to be a Type One greeting life with customary enthusiasm. Innovators or stubborn die-hards, whimsical, demanding, moody – children of the New Moon are hard to ignore. When they were born the Moon was beginning to move away from the Sun at the commencement of a fresh cycle. This phase corresponds to the most childlike (but that does not mean child*ish*) the most basic, and in some ways the most dynamic stirrings of consciousness. Growth is just starting, as if the green shoot is about to pierce the surface of the soil, so this is a time for beginnings, but also of knowledge of roots and the soil of origin. This is reflected in the instinctual nature of Ones, who need both to be breaking new ground and maintaining contact with their base, to feel comfortable. This is the 'waxing' time of waxing. We usually visualise the Goddess as adult, so this phase corresponds to her as Maiden, on the very threshold of puberty, fresh, vibrant and excited.

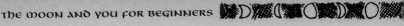

New Moons are avid for experience. Life is not always easy for them, for they are destined to usher in the untried and untested almost whether they like it or not, and in so doing often encounter opposition, if not incomprehension from others. They may come with their loins girded for a fight, but they rarely tilt at windmills. Often assertive but seldom aggressive without extreme provocation, they prefer to gain acceptance by a flash of their sudden smile. They are not above stirring up a little conflict, however. Things must be kept moving, people must be kept on their toes and boredom must be averted at all costs!

These people are both self-indulgent and caring, possessive yet champions of freedom. Sentimental iconoclasts, spontaneous, affectionate, yet detached – they are full of contradictions. The trendy New Moon executive, tapping away at his laptop computer may wear a gold band on his little finger, and may tell you, moist-eyed, that it belonged to his great-aunt Alice. Many New Moons embody a quaint combination of the avant-garde with the time-honoured. There is a perpetual two-way pull for New Moons, footsteps on unexplored paths yet overshadowed by family and history. This dilemma is most marked if the Moon is very new, in her first day. New Moons are not prone to agonise over contradictions, however, and many are as comfortable with history as with science fiction.

In the guise of total rebellion a young New Moon may display a dogmatism to rival the most fearsome patriarch! None the less, authority is probably secretly admired. Type Ones may emulate it behind a cunning disguise of doing exactly the opposite.

It is important to remember that the Moon has to do with nurturing, both of the self and others. In Type One people these energies are unrefined, and can sometimes find comical expression. One unsuspecting woman found herself in a whirlwind romance with a New Moon man. In the fashion of his phase, having decided what he wanted, he went after it single-mindedly and she was charmed by his faith in their future and the refreshing enthusiasm with which he went about organising it. Within six months of their meeting they were ensconced in a new home, mortgage in place and baby on the way. However, she soon discovered that his instinctive way of

protecting his security was to hoard anything and everything. She had dismissed the thicket of boxes and unidentifiable objects in which he had formerly lived as the poor housekeeping of a bachelor, but her amusement gave way to horror when the full extent of his possessions became evident. She still wonders why anyone could need six umbrellas or thirty empty cardboard boxes. Nor is he able to tell her.

Of course, not all Type Ones look after themselves by hoarding. The opposite side of the coin can come up in frequent sort-outs (though they'll usually keep a few bits and pieces 'in case'). Some forge on with the New in a more physical fashion. The parents of one New Moon boy were driven to distraction by his determination to be always as far from them as possible, from the time he could crawl. At the age of nine months he climbed out of his playpen in three lithe movements. The expression on his face said, 'Could have done that weeks ago'. Three months later he was found missing from the back garden, despite the special gate that had been installed as a restraint. Running down the road, his frantic mother glimpsed the small white blob of his nappy disappearing into the distance. Years later he launched himself into his first day at school without even a wave. However, with true New Moon ambiguity he possesses a home-loving streak. Now a teenager, there is only one thing he likes doing better than cooking delicious meals for the family – eating them! Although they may hate to be stuck at home, Type Ones like to know the way back is always open.

New Moon antennae are perpetually a-tremble to pick up data on anything and everything – often they are veritable info-holics. Mostly they are fashionably dressed and *au fait* with the current terminology. Many love technology, or at least the latest ideas appeal, if not the latest gadgets and hardware. Not every New Moon is a computer expert, but they tend to prize computer literacy, and given half the chance they will be reaching round the globe on the Information Superhighway.

Travelling holds a never-ending fascination for Type Ones. If they are also Ariens or Sagittarians, you may find – or perhaps lose – them in the upper reaches of the Amazon. Of course the comfort-loving New

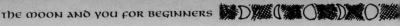

Moon can easily degenerate into a couch potato, but be sure they are armchair travellers at least, following the Silk Road to Samarkand. Many New Moons have a love of fantasy and/or science fiction.

Many New Moon males are out and out New Men – almost. Having a woman boss can fit in well with their ideas that existing structures are continually up for review, and they can be supportive to the careers of their wives. Deep down, however, there is a part of them that likes to see tradition observed. A female boss is fine within an established hierarchy (probably designed originally by men) and a successful wife is great as long as the roles are not completely swapped if children arrive. New Moon men are rarely quite laid back enough, or committed enough to their belief in the New to take readily to the role of house-husband. New Moon women, however, must have a career. They will hang on to a good measure of autonomy and independence, and while they may accept the need to stay at home if they have small children, they will make sure the back door is always open. Both sexes have a constant need for stimulation, and will usually look for this in the company of other people. Both males and females secretly prefer to set up home close to their parents.

New Moon people are enthusiastic and energetic carers, noticing details about the creature comforts of their loved ones with an almost uncanny perceptiveness. It is the New Moon who will always be there at the door ahead of you, ready to usher you through in comfort. You can rely on a New Moon to carry your bags (male or female) and have the kettle on the boil when you come in from the rain – that is, if they like you! If they don't they may not even notice that you are there, and you'll be lucky to find the tea-bags. The generosity of New Moons is rivalled only by their meanness when the mood takes them.

In Type One people, born when the Moon energies are formative, the ways of looking after the self may be extreme, or unusual. A New Moon person whose childhood has been stressful is more likely than many to comfort him/herself with alcohol or drugs, and the New Moons who haven't had their childhood quota of caring are

unlikely to suffer in silence as adults. They can be extremely demanding and easily provoked to resentment. Even a well-balanced New Moon will typically display some excessive or quixotic form or self-nurture, such as overeating, buying binges or hoarding, as we have seen. When they realise they have gone over the top, they may then go to the other extreme of austerity, only to revert at some later stage to self-indulgence once more. Type Ones do need to moderate their behaviour, and to realise that their real needs are not being met by their excesses, for only by asking themselves what those are can they find true security.

Perhaps the greatest appeal of Type Ones is the infectious way they enjoy themselves. Greedy they can be, but they are usually big-hearted too. Most people find that even their greed has its charm, accompanied as it usually is by indulgence of their companions. A New Moon who has achieved a reasonable degree of inner security has a great deal to give.

RELATIONSHIPS

To relationships, as to all else, New Moon people bring an enthusiasm second to none. If one of them has decided that you are the one he or she wants, they will stop at nothing – almost – to get you. This can be very exciting. A New Moon partner can conjure up a vision of a brilliant new life, not because of anything they may do or promise, but because of their infectious zest for the partnership and life in general. No one is more romantic than a New Moon on the track of love. Partners can expect candlelit dinners, deluges of flowers and long, late-night phone calls. It must have been a New Moon making sure that the lady got her Milk Tray!

The new/old dichotomy is present in relationships also, for New Moons. Itching to escape the dry and dusty they may break hearts and conventions. Often they will marry the most unlikely person, seemingly chosen specifically to shock parents and to mystify friends, but tradition stalks them. Somehow they end up being conventional after all. Sometimes they choose partners who will seem to break the rules for them. A middle-class New Moon girl

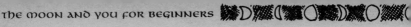

may marry her tatooed Hell's Angel boyfriend rather than living with him – and, dare we say it, she might be a virgin on her wedding night!

What sort of partner does the New Moon make? Eccentric, irritating, cuddly, fussy, moody, affectionate, attentive, sometimes remote, often charming and very caring, New Moons are an unpredictable mixture. Will they be faithful? Well ... maybe. New Moons don't really relish the discomfort of infidelity, but neither can they bear to feel shackled. To cope with a New Moon partner you had better have a life and identity of your own, and you had better not be boring. Supply them with something eternally fresh (they probably chose you for your capacity to do that anyway) and your New Moon will remain happily at your side, for the most part. Become too predictable and they'll feel compelled to escape, albeit temporarily. Get a little erratic yourself and you'll usually know where you are with your New Moon. New Moons can be jealous, and it may be a good idea to arouse this side of them sometimes, just in a playful way. Broody though they may be, few New Moons are likely to turn into Othellos, and knowing someone else fancies you can keep them on their toes – and they're usually happier that way.

Sexuality is a subtle matter, but we can make some good guesses about how it will express itself on the basis of the phase of the Moon at birth. New Moons are often easily seduced, initially. All things being equal, their responses are quick and simple, and they tend towards ardour rather than tortured passion, although they can be deeply hurt by deceit. In this area, too, New Moons seem to have more than one face. If you meet your New Moon in his or her adventurous mode – which will usually prove the case at the start of the relationship, you can throw away your copy of the *Kama Sutra*. Not that they are likely to have taken the time to read it, although they might have written it if they could have been bothered!

Some New Moons can find sex in public a turn-on. One secretary, excited by the advances of her boss behind the steamy windows of his Porsche (New Moons like flashy cars), found that she had to draw the line at his intention to take matters further across the bonnet in a quiet (but not quiet enough!) country lane. Probably it

is the raw simplicity of al fresco sex that can appeal to New Moons. Mostly, however, they opt for comfort in this area, as with most others.

With their penchant for the untried, one might expect New Moons to enjoy the very unconventional. This tends rarely to be the case, however. Though they may enjoy pornography, and three in a bed may be a good game, some things are quite distasteful to them. Of course, any early damage will affect New Moons as much as the next person. Generally, however, the innocence of New Moons asserts itself. At heart they are fairly uncomplicated souls – and let us not forget the voice of Tradition, whispering in their ear as their lover nibbles the lobe! In the long run New Moons feel that the best place for sex is the marriage bed, and it's quite nice to produce children although preferably not 2.4 arriving on schedule. Again, the risk at some point is boredom, and if you are married to a New Moon try some spice rather than sugar!

New Moons make admirable spouses in many ways. They are thoughtful, and though they may be quite thin on empathy – except in a Cancer, Pisces or Scorpio – they are responsive with the sympathy. Your New Moon may not have a clue what you're feeling deep down. They often lack complexity, and the dark emotions overshadowing some hearts are foreign territory to them. But if you need to cry, their shoulder will always be available, and if the car won't start they will be under the bonnet or on the phone to the garage before you have time to get frustrated. With a New Moon, life is fairly cosy, and also unpredictable, and if that seems like a contradiction it is also the very stuff of which New Moons are made.

FAMILY LIFE

Eternal infants at heart, New Moon parents are especially in tune with the playfulness of youngsters. The New Moon mum joins in the wonderment of her child's perspective on life, getting on all fours with him, rolling over, giggling – play will be more important to her than nappy-changing. The New Moon dad, making appalling faces at his offspring is amusing himself as much as his baby.

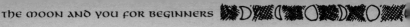

New Moons are usually good at seeing things from the position of a small child, and they can identify deeply with a baby's need to be cuddled and fed. Although they may never have seen themselves as parents, New Moons often take to it like a duck to water. Nothing is too much trouble for the new arrival, and New Moons often expend a great part of their not inconsiderable energy in ensuring the comfort of their child. There is something in the enquiring gaze of the new baby that answers something in their very soul, and they are speedily entranced by the magical process of life renewing itself.

While their children are small, New Moon parents can be great fun, always thinking up new games, and entering into them with as much pleasure as the child. The lust for life of the New Moon tends to keep them from being too squeamish about a little healthy muck, and so most of these parents can see the funny side when jam goes in the ear, or hits the wall – and dirty nappies don't phase them. After all, changing a nappy is yet another game, with lots of silly noises and funny faces.

The extravagant side of the New Moon is likely to be stimulated by parenthood, and the house may be cluttered with brightly coloured bricks and cuddly bunnies. It is quite possible for the children of New Moons to be somewhat overwhelmed, and they may become grown-up at an early age, especially if they were born when the Moon was waning. After all, someone has to act like an adult, and if Mum and Dad won't, the child may reason that he or she should. In reasonably well-balanced families this will all take place on a superficial level, however, for New Moons make as responsible parents as anyone else. Their children are certainly likely to embark upon life as if it were an exciting adventure.

Many New Moons are ideally suited to bringing up young children. It is when they are somewhat older that things may progress less smoothly. In some ways, of all the phases the New Moon has the least patience. Babies and toddlers do not frustrate them because they understand them. However, unco-operative teenagers can send then into orbit! If Billy's football has shattered his New Moon mum's best china, or Katie has scratched Dad's new car with the handlebars of her bike, they had better hide. New Moon anger tends to be swift and electric, but happily short-lived.

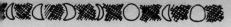

These days many people find themselves in step-families, and these can be a mixed blessing for New Moons. On the one hand a ready-made family can provide someone to play with, and if stepchildren share the interests of their parent's new spouse they can all be good friends very quickly. New Moons can be readily irritated, however, by competition for attention, and it may at times be difficult to tell which is the child and which is the adult, as each lays claim to the black cherry yogurt. Fortunately New Moons are ready to explore different ways to solve such dilemmas and their sense of humour will usually reassert itself. New Moon stepchildren are likely to give their new parent a good chance. They may think it's 'cool' to have two mums or two dads and they are not slow to spot the possible financial advantages. They are less likely than some phases to agonise over divided loyalties.

New Moon children are particularly adventurous, and can be so avid for new experiences that they seem never really to take anything in. They need to be encouraged to slow down and to realise that in trying to absorb everything they are in fact absorbing very little, and that their worst fear – that of missing something – is in fact a perpetual reality. Their overloaded systems tend to shut down, and all they are doing is buzzing around rather like spinning tops. They need to be reminded to be selective. It is their instinct to seek stimulation, and that will not change, but they must be encouraged to let some experiences roll off them and others to take root.

For the most part they are responsive and charming youngsters, very affectionate and cuddly as infants, open and forthcoming as teenagers. There will often be a special toy or 'security blanket' that follows them through early childhood. Often they appear confident and extrovert (although some prefer solitary adventures) and their excursions can extend into any area – intellectual, emotional, physical, according to the rest of their temperament.

Intellect is indicated by chart factors other than Moon phase, but it can be said that most New Moons catch on quickly within their familiar sphere. New Moon parents may be impatient of a child who is slow or dreamy. They aspire to achievement of some sort for their

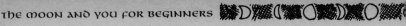

offspring, at school or in groups, and as time goes by they tend to look for a measure of conformity. Having no doubt flouted parental authority in their own youth, they like to see their offspring involved in something respectable. They will think up all sorts of good reasons why young Johnny shouldn't busk on the street corner, but the real reasons are that no one in the family has ever done it before, and they really wanted to do it themselves.

In the long run, however, New Moon parents try to support their children, and after the initial rows often enter into the excitement of their enterprises. This can be great – or not. It's not quite the same going to a rave if your New Moon mum or dad chauffeurs you there.

CAREER

Their future is something that most New Moons dream about a great deal, from an early age. From astronaut to master-chef their ambitions are varied and changeable, but usually involve breaking new ground. As adults they are prone to job changes – not always by conscious choice – and they, of all the phases, are the most likely to contemplate a fresh start even quite late in life.

'The grass is always greener on the other side of the fence', and 'Fresh fields and pastures new', are phrases that could have been penned by Type Ones. Their behaviour might be considered irresponsible by the more hidebound, but if you examine their actions carefully you will notice that this is rarely the case. New Moons don't relish insecurity, and while they will put up with it on the trail of something exciting, they will rarely mortgage hearth and home for some hare-brained scheme.

Talents are only slightly hinted at by Moon phase, so you will find New Moons in all walks of life. They need freedom, however, as they need air, and if their occupation doesn't give them these then they are sure to be scanning the Situations Vacant pages each week, looking for a way out. Once they have found it they will spread their wings and be off without a backward glance. Until they have an alternative, however, they are unlikely just to walk out and plunge themselves into insecurity. Suitable work for a New Moon involves

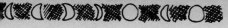

variety and novelty. Travel that appeals can be mental or physical, but it is often the latter – New Moons take well to jobs as reps. Staying overnight in hotels appeals to them, and moving from contact to contact, making friends with many but getting close to few, suits them fine.

When choosing a job, New Moons need to check out the scope for mobility, both upwardly and laterally. Generally New Moons are quite ambitious, but that is not everything. A sideways move can be very attractive if it means fresh stimulation. A New Moon trapped in a dull 9 to 5 is as sad as a lark in a cage, and all the more so because only in the most extreme circumstances do they feel able to throw it all away without an alternative already set up – and that is becoming harder and harder to do. Instead they are more likely to stay put, playing picador with the sacred cows and bickering with the die-hards of middle management. Give them some new ground to cultivate and there is no one happier, but they are a liability when constrained.

Having their own business can be ideal for New Moons, for they have the vision to project themselves into the business world of tomorrow – after all 'tomorrow' is their eternal destination. Again, they will avoid excessive risk, and often taking a franchise in some newly established concern can prove a workable option. New Moons tend to be physically and/or mentally energetic, but they need to be sure that the type of activity involved is compatible with their aptitudes.

These New Moons need to be careful with their budgeting – they know this quite well, but somehow rarely manage it! Attracted, butterfly-like to anything novel or pretty, they find many things almost irresistible, and their impulsiveness can get them into deeper debt than can be salvaged by a sudden stingy fad. Ways need to be found to turn saving from a drag into a game. Some New Moons like to buy premium bonds, so they can keep open the possibility of a windfall while retaining their money. Others like to dabble on the stockmarket. They will rarely risk their shirt, but their indestructible faith in life imbues them with the secret belief that lady luck will smile on them one day – and often she does.

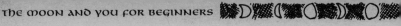

New Moons' love of 'the latest' will be evident in the way they manage their career, and they are likely to feel thwarted if they cannot drive the most up-to-date car and be in touch with state-of-the-art technology. If they are of a more abstract temperament they will want to feel in the forefront of ideas. They need to be in touch with the latest that civilisation has to offer. They must stand forever poised at the portal of Tomorrow, or they feel – and are – displaced. It is their role in life to usher in the future and to 'sell' it to the less imaginative. To do this effectively they must always be able to blend it with the tried and tested – they are not people to throw the baby out with the bathwater.

New Moons are great communicators, and they are usually salesmen – of themselves, an idea or philosophy. Their task is to usher in the New on the foundations of the Old and come to terms with the dilemmas this entails. It is not an easy task to decide what should be salvaged, what modified and what left behind. Most of us can ignore this, but for New Moons, at a level that may be barely conscious or totally unconscious, this is a dilemma on the horns of which they are perpetually balanced. Others may find their ways exasperating, threatening, eccentric or hilarious, but theirs is the new vision of civilisation, without which we might not have progressed far from our ancestral caves.

MAKING THE BEST OF YOURSELF

If you are a typical Type One, chances are that you've turned to this page avid for more information about yourself that you can do something useful with. As we saw in the section on 'Family Life', one of the traps you often fall into is the Flat Spin condition, where there is an awful lot of movement, but very little being achieved – like the headless chicken, or, more colourfully, a Catherine Wheel. Sparks may go off in all directions, but the ending is a fizzle.

Of course I do have some advice for you, and that is that you erect some boundaries around yourself. Give yourself some blinkers. Or imagine that you're a climbing plant, perhaps a honeysuckle, and instead of trailing off in all directions you have been trained to grow

one or two ways only. It may be that you are so afraid of missing anything, be it people, events or information, that you are often overloaded and really miss having a deep experience of anything. Some things just have to go. This will be painful at first, but after a while it will be so much more comfortable – and you know how you like comfort. Also, you will find that you get so much more done and feel so much more 'on the ball' that you won't feel you're missing out. You are probably an intense person, so focus that intensity.

If you are a bogged-down New Moon who can't seem to pierce the topsoil, you need a fresh energy-source, like a plant needs a few sunny days to establish growth. You may have been looking about for stimulation – perhaps in all sorts of places – but nothing seems to get you going or give you feeling of animation. Perhaps all these experiences have been glancing off the smooth walls of your depression. Stand back and work out, by simple logic if inspiration is stubborn, what ought to get you going, and do it. After a while your interest will be truly stimulated, but if that doesn't happen after a reasonable interval, scrap the plan for another, but keep trying. Don't be manic, but be thorough. Do not be afraid to try something completely different – and I mean *completely*. Search around for what you have never dreamt of doing, and do it! Of course you won't want to bungee jump if you're afraid of heights, but anything, anywhere, anyhow that doesn't actually repel is worth a try. Think of yourself as an explorer – get out and find out. It is your instinct to initiate, and you cannot do this by keeping still, apart from sensible pauses for reflection. Keep your spirits up. Sooner or later you will find your niche.

COMPATIBILITIES

Ones can be good with Nines, for below the surface they do have things in common and can complement each other, although Ones may feel overshadowed, and Nines insecure in the partnership. Ones and Sevens can be dynamic, Threes and Eights are likely to irritate them. Twos may be 'a bit much'. Fives and Sixes can attract and achieve a feeling of balance.

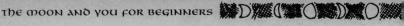

VISUALISATION

You are standing in the shadow of a dolmen – three large stones supporting a fourth, that forms a roof over you. The stones are at the top of a rounded hill, but you are sheltered from all breezes, and are in shadow. There is a sweet smell of dampness, moss and antiquity, and there is a feeling of peace.

You step out from beneath the dolmen and see that it is early morning. There is a faint glow of dawn in the East, but the rest of the sky is still purple. A gentle breeze touches your cheek, coming from the direction of the sunrise. It is clean and fresh, but not in the least bit cold.

You begin moving down the slope towards the sunrise and as you do the musical sound of splashing water reaches you. In the middle of a clump of saplings you discover a silver fountain rising from the centre of a clear pool.

Now you may like to take your shoes off and paddle in this pool, or you may be daring and take off all your clothes and stand beneath the crystal fountain. No one can see you; you are perfectly safe. Remember, the water is fresh, but not cold. It is comfortable to the touch, smooth and pure. Moisten your forehead with it. Feel it clearing your mind, giving you energy, fresh enthusiasm and joy in life.

Affirm to yourself, 'I am fresh and new. Full of ideas, I am a pioneer.' Repeat this three times.

Now you may slowly return to everyday consciousness, or you may follow the small stream that runs eastward from the pool, and see where it leads – in a sort of waking dream. What you find may be interesting – if it is write it down when you come round. When you decide to finish your journey, imagine yourself back by the pool, and then come back to everyday awareness.

OTHER TYPE ONES

Bruce Springsteen, Annie Lennox, Howard Sasportas (astrologer)
Igor Stravinsky, Thomas Hardy, Muhammad Ali, Ringo Starr, Roy
Orbison, Madonna, D. H. Lawrence.

EARTHLY HARMONIES

Colours   Silver, white, pale and bright blue, most bright colours.
Occasionally scarlet. Sometimes deep moss-green.
Oils, flowers, herbs   Lemon, lemon balm, bergamot mint,
peppermint, pine, lavender.
Stones   Beryl, pearl, red or mottled jasper, agate.

CHAPTER 4

TYPE TWO:
INNOCENTS AND
EAGER BEAVERS

*I love to rise in a summer morn
When the birds sing on every tree;
The distant huntsman winds his horn
And the skylark sings with me.*

William Blake, 'The Schoolboy'

Noses pressed to the grindstone or raised hopefully in the morning light, these people are avid, alive and busy, busy, busy. They rarely enjoy sitting still. Instead they prefer to make things happen, and usually this can only be accomplished by action. However, they are also capable of stirring things up by words and ideas when occasion demands. This is the woman who is always arranging flowers, or knitting – when she is not at a board meeting. It is the man whose home stands evidence to his ceaseless DIY projects – which moreover he generally finishes – in between sales conferences and rounds of golf.

If this makes you feel a bit dizzy, that is certainly not the effect that Type Twos create. There is no whirlwind around them. Rather they seem relaxed and to have plenty of time, and it's only by observation and putting two and two together that you realise how dynamic they are and how much they achieve. They seem usually to be poised on the brink of something, and yet their presence can be quite soothing. If you have a problem, are unwell or need help, then this is where to come for it. Type Twos love to be needed and they will engage gear smoothly and roll into action.

In terms of the Moon's cycle the initial stage of first beginnings and

their attendant doubts and ambivalence is past. Now growth is well under way, and although there may be a certain tremulousness at the sheer range of possibilities on offer, there is also a feeling of getting into 'stride'. In picturing the Goddess aspect, now is the 'Full' time of Waxing – nubile Maiden, confident in her power and conscious of her potential. The instincts of those born at this time are to move forward, get going, explore, and they have their eyes set on what they can accomplish and create. To some extent their feeling of inner security depends on keeping active and productive – they tend to feel 'at home' if they are busy. They respond to stimuli by going into action. Potentials, opportunities, avenues for expansion all pass before their inner eye in a flash, often unconsciously, but they are not prone to ponder. They select their path automatically, and get moving.

It has to be said that sometimes they do interfere – just a little bit! They usually believe that they know all the best ways of going about things, and feel that it's only fair to give you the benefit of their expertise! Of course this can be irritating, but Twos are so efficient that they are worth listening to. Better still, let them get on with it themselves. They will love that, as long as they aren't taken for granted.

Of course, not all Twos are practical people – but they are always active people, and if this isn't evident it's certainly going on within. Their minds are driving forward, they have plans and ideas – places to go, people to see, even if these are sometimes theoretical. Often they are original, and at their best they are inspired. They can be great to be around because their simplicity and enthusiasm is infectious, and can make one feel that anything is possible.

Twos have a boundless faith in life. They are excited by possibilities and prepared to open new doors just for the sake of it. They are eager for adventure, but they do not see life as a challenge so much as a vast range of opportunities. 'Tomorrow is another day' has a very real meaning for them.

The faith of Twos often extends to the spiritual. Obviously this phase does not have the monopoly on religion, but there is a simplicity in them that often translates into a form of worship. This

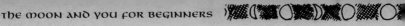

need not be specifically Christian. There can be a childlike quality in Twos that grabs at a belief system like a baton to run with. They are rarely dogmatic but they may be just a little evangelical, if fired up. If they believe something, they will use it as a background to their life. In this they are sometimes a touch gullible, but really that is neither here nor there. 'If it feels good, do it' is their maxim.

Two also have faith in themselves. Deep within they carry the conviction that the world is their oyster waiting to yield its pearls, as they gently, relentlessly prise them out. This faith can give them immense strength. One cancer patient, diagnosed as having a particularly malignant form of the disease, was given six months to live. Two and a half years later he was still going strong, trying all treatments from homeopathy to hypnotherapy, but above all believing in himself. 'It's not my time to die,' he told me, running a hand through the hair that intensive chemotherapy had hardly harmed. Another Two, prone on a hospital bed after a back injury, was told that she would probably never walk again. A year later she was digging the garden. It is not so much that Twos are determined not to be beaten, though of course they may be. Their strength derives more from a conviction that they are the indomitable Children of the Gods.

There is a wonderment in life for Twos that makes the mythological out of the mundane, and if 'real life' isn't quite exciting enough they may take steps to pep it up. Fantasy games often appeal, as they do to Eights, but Twos are more keen to 'live' the fantasy consciously and actively. Joining something like 'Sealed Knot' and re-enacting the dramas of Cavalier and Roundhead can be just the thing for Twos, engaging their inventiveness in all sorts of ways.

Generally speaking Twos believe in working hard and playing hard. After grafting six and half days a week all year, the sedate may decide to caravan on the Continent for a month or so, while the more adventurous take a bike ride to China or swim with the dolphins. Holidays are often important to Twos and they like an absorbing and stimulating change. Usually they are fascinated by foreign countries, and more introverted Twos are beguiled by the diversity of ideas from other cultures. It often seems to them that

there aren't enough hours in the day or days in the year for all they want to experience.

It may sound as if Twos inhabit a Disney world, where everyone lives happily ever after (except the wicked witch) and flattened cats re-inflate to chase the same grinning cartoon mouse. However, like everyone else they have their darker side, and this can be harder to cope with because they are often so persistent about ignoring it. Sometimes they can be insincere and careless, or at least that's how it seems. They don't lack depth, but they prefer to gaze at the sun-kissed peaks rather than the shadowed valley. Thus they do not always understand their own motives and may wax indignant when accused of selfishness, envy or duplicity, of which they can be as guilty as the rest of us. They can need emotional care-taking, especially if the signs of Cancer, Scorpio and Pisces are lacking.

Twos are impulsive and open. They seldom expect to meet with unpleasant reactions, and so they can be vulnerable. Often they are deeply hurt and puzzled by aggression or spite, although they may have provoked it. There is a sensitive side to them and they may be easily moved to tears. Usually, however, they bounce back, and some enthusiastically repeat the same mistakes time and again!

When things do get them down – and it sometimes takes an awful lot – they can hit rock bottom and it can be a hard job to dredge them up. When angry they are not easy to pacify, and their depressions are the blackest of black. This is not a 'spoilt child' reaction, but at some level an incomprehension that things just haven't worked for them. They often need help to understand this and themselves.

RELATIONSHIPS

With Twos one can sometimes get a 'two-dimensional' feeling, as if one is a character in a play that they are choreographing. This can be disconcerting, and can leave one high and dry when seeking empathy. But it can also be exciting. Twos don't expect to write the script alone, and in a play anything can happen. Often they see the relationship as a replay of Arthurian romance, or some such, and it

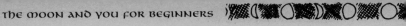

can seem as if they are not totally immersed in it. There is a part of them watching the action, even while they are taking part. This may be anything but obvious, and all one may sense is that they are not entirely 'there'. This is not quite true – it's just that it's hard to be 'all present and correct' when your mind is ranging over such a variety of possibilities. However, if you want to talk about the bridesmaids' dresses or the colour of the new carpet they will enter into it happily enough. Just don't take too long to decide!

In general, Twos work very hard at relationships and do their best to please their lover. If you're ill they'll sort out the washing, feed the dogs and call in at the Supermarket on the way to work. If you want to plan and dream they will sit by the fire and do it with you. If you have a busy life of your own they will be quite happy to let you get on with it. However, if you are deeply troubled about something that's complicated or hard to express they can be mystified. They are likely to cover this mystification (and conceal it from themselves, if they can) by being bright and breezy, examining the subject from all angles and rounding it all off with a 'Cheer up, love!'

One woman, married to a Two man, felt very divided on the subject of having children. She was in her early thirties, with a high-powered job as a buyer, so pregnancy would mean a loss of status, occupation and money, which would not be readily retrieved. On the other hand she was aware that the 'biological clock' was ticking. She and her husband discussed this from all angles. He worked out how they would manage, and gave many suggestions as to what she could do to keep in the swing of things after the birth, offering to look after the baby while she did them. What he was quite unable to do was to understand her deep ambivalence about motherhood – that it was something she both longed for with every nerve and was scared rigid by. Each month brought hopes, fears and tears. Finally he found her convulsed with sobs over a little test-tube that confirmed her pregnancy. It was too much! He slammed out of the house; she was mortally hurt. A year later they have a lovely baby girl and share busy lives, but she has learnt to appreciate his tireless help and to look elsewhere for empathy.

Twos are not insensitive. They care very much when someone is

upset and it really bothers them if they cannot put it right. They are 'fixers' and if they can't get results they will leave the scene, not because they're hard-hearted but because the frustration is too much to bear. Twos also often like to play Cupid. They get a kick out of matchmaking among their friends and are not above a little scheming to bring couples together. If you are single and a Two invites you to a party it should not be difficult to spot your intended partner. Do try not to be insulted if it's someone you wouldn't be seen dead with. The Two will have made the selection on the basis of the best in each of you, not your faults.

These people are capable of falling deeply and passionately in love and of committing themselves with a simple devotion. They often do not see complications and can be equally blind to faults. Not especially prone to jealousy they do not expect it in their partners – although less so if Scorpio, Cancer, Capricorn or Taurus are present. Sometimes they can seem a little selfish. They can't see why they shouldn't have what they want, and they take things at face value, which can lead to trouble.

One Type Two woman, bored with her long-term relationship (which, however, she had no intention of quitting) became deeply infatuated with a married man. Her own partner, although considering himself free to flirt, vetoed any such action for her. Make no mistake, if treated unfairly Twos will feel free to deceive. She began an affair with the man, whose wife – amazingly – went out of the house taking the children, so they could make their trysts. All was progressing fine. She was enjoying herself and it didn't occur to her that anything might be seething under the surface, until the worm turned, and the wronged wife venomously 'shopped' her to her suspicious husband. Twos don't always appreciate that a person's behaviour may not reflect their true feelings.

Twos resemble Ones in their attitude to sex. Mostly they are healthy 'straight' people, and while their libido may be strong there can be just a touch of what some would call prudery in them. They may regard themselves as extremely liberated, and when it comes to enjoying themselves they are, but anything 'weird' puts them off. Twos get a tremendous kick from being good lovers, for in love as in

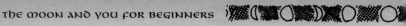

anything else, to them 'a thing worth doing is worth doing well'. They are capable of retaining their sexuality into advanced years. 'Use it or lose it' is their maxim.

family life

Families can place great demands on energy, but Twos are usually equal to the challenge. They rather like the fact that they can keep several balls in the air at once. Female Twos will happily switch hats from cook to teacher, to nurse, to accountant, to whatever. They can cope with house, job, children and hobbies seamlessly. The men are similar, and can usually be relied upon to take their turn with nappies and dishes.

It may seem that Twos have endless energy, but the truth is they have little more than the rest of us. What they are good at is not wasting it. Although they may take on a lot they draw the line where they can cope. They are often instinctive planners, having a good idea how long each job will take. Also they like a varied, busy life. When something is enjoyed it is experienced as easy. Sometimes one may wonder, however, if Twos like to keep busy because it prevents them from having to reflect on anything unpleasant. Twos may say, virtuously, 'The Devil makes work for idle hands', but being constantly occupied can be a way of escape. Some Twos really are running away from the realisation that they aren't perfect, and this can be difficult for their children, who may have a lot to live up to.

As parents, Twos are great fun, with plenty of time to tie shoelaces and give a push on the swings. Like Ones they can relate to the child's freshness of outlook. For the young, the world is created anew each day, and Twos retain this feeling into advanced age. Twos do expect effort and co-operation from their children. This can work well at first, but when the child develops a mind and preferences of their own (and these may be for the life of a couch-potato) the Two's incomprehension can amount to condemnation. Twos are usually so inspiring and interesting as parents that life is eternally stimulating for the child, but some teenagers, as we all know quite well, won't co-operate at any price. Having such a busy parent can be 'a bit much'

and the teenage children of Twos may respond with loutish indifference. Nothing is more calculated to drive a Type Two into an uncharacteristic beating of the brow, asking themselves where they've gone wrong. It is hard for Twos, striving to do their best, to realise that they need to learn to listen to their offspring, and try to understand their perspective.

Many Twos are tidy, even if only in mind. The children's rooms are typically chock-a-block with books, models and the latest half-finished project. Often they like to have some state-of-the-art technology at their disposal. A Two child may one minute be completely occupied building a replica of the Starship Enterprise, and the next be standing on a chair squealing in fright at a spider. Once the crisis is past, the youngster becomes speedily absorbed again. Twos often prefer to forget or ignore anything unpleasant, both inside them and outside. This is often fairly easy, as there is so much about them that truly is harmonious. It doesn't help them to cope the next time a spider crawls out, however!

Many people remember their teenage years as a type of hell, but Twos come into their own at this age. That bit of extra independence, the strength of approaching adulthood, and the wider range of possibilities now open to them is very exciting. They may get involved in local schemes and at their best can be helpful. If they appear to have their future sorted out, don't be deceived. They need as much help as the next adolescent, although they may already be learning how to give the impression of coping.

When it comes to step-families, Twos prefer to get on with life. They don't often agonise over their own or anyone else's ex-partner, unless they are making themselves a nuisance. Then they will attempt to deal with the situation with a heavy tact that may make things worse! If step-siblings promise to be enthusiastic playmates they are likely to be welcomed. Twos usually accept step-parents, as long as they seem to like them and want to play with them. They don't expect bitterness among the adults, and will be impervious to it unless their noses are rubbed in it.

Because Twos are so civilised, they can give great pleasure to their families. Inventive and playful, they can turn Christmas or a birthday

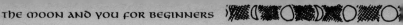

into a real celebration by entering thoroughly into the spirit of the occasion. They prefer to ignore any negative undercurrents, believing that if you ignore them they will go away – and it sometimes works.

CAREER

These people are full of schemes but are often prepared to take the future as it comes. As you might expect, the average Two makes an excellent employee, prepared to work very hard and put in overtime if required, occasionally without pay. This will depend on how much a Two enjoys their work – and they won't be doing it long if they don't like it. It is also important to them to feel appreciated. Twos often have a healthy opinion of their own worth. They need to feel valued for their efforts. However, proper thanks and a judicious 'Goodness, have you really done all that!' will go a long way, and enable you to continue to benefit from their industry – if you can put up with their smug expression.

They can be a little conceited and maddeningly impervious to any attempt to 'take them down a peg'. Try it and they may regard you with a mild, indulgent contempt. There is something innocent about both their disdain and big-headedness, however, so they rarely cause much offence. Twos often achieve promotion after promotion, without apparent effort. They have an instinct for being in the right place at the right time. There is the occasional Two that feels the world owes him/her a living, while they industriously pursue their hobbies, and this will apply to a Two who has in some way been 'spoilt' as a child. However, this is infrequent. Any Two who is unhappy at work will not put up with it for long. They are capable of walking out, blissfully secure in the confidence that something else will turn up – and it usually does! Twos' faith in life is often rewarded.

When choosing a career Twos need to bear in mind that it is important to them to feel useful. They need variety and a sensation of always going somewhere, although they are not excessively ambitious. Productiveness is important to them. Jetting off to meetings in Paris and Brussels will swiftly pall for them if they don't feel much is being achieved. Twos are often suited to a literal 'helping' profession, such as nursing, at which they will graft tirelessly.

Running their own business can be attractive to Twos. They have the confidence to believe that difficulties can be overcome and the persistence needed to do so. However, they may underestimate obstacles and their own capacity for hitting the deck when overwhelmed, so a well-chosen partner is to be recommended. Twos make good partners, for they remind themselves that they must consider the other person's point of view, although they can go about this in a way that is cumbersome and patronising. They do not insist on their own way, although they often get it.

Twos are well aware of the value of money and 'cut their coat according to their cloth'. They are not exactly mean, but they are not often overwhelmed by generous impulses either. They like to feel they can see themselves and their dependants through a crisis, and will provide for this. However, they are not obsessed with pension schemes, believing that they can cross that bridge when they come to it, which they generally do fairly nimbly.

It may sound as if Twos skim over the surface of life like waterflies, and for some Twos this may be true. Twos are concerned with potentials rather than implications. They are more interested in where they are going than where they have come from, and after all if you are looking downwards and backwards on your flight you are sure to bump into something. Twos do need to remember that things are not always what they seem. None the less they can show us all the value of positive thinking and how to regard our glasses as half full, not half empty.

MAKING THE BEST OF YOURSELF

If you were born a Type Two you may well feel that you're doing your best anyway. However, it may be helpful to remind yourself that although you may believe you're right, you may not have all the relevant facts – even if it seems that you have. Your instincts are usually healthy, but you may oversimplify and there may be some things that you just haven't seen. This isn't a matter of not having your eyes open, for you are usually observant. However, you may be blinded by the light. You may not see shadows or the things that shift in them.

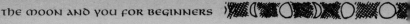

To help you, you need all your imagination and a dash of humility. Subtlety is something you may have to work at. People and their feelings are infinitely varied, so never think that you have it all worked out. It's quite all right if you don't understand certain aspects of yourself or others, but it is important to admit it. If you can accept that there are nuances you tend to miss, you are more likely to start picking them up. If you realise that there are bits of yourself you are denying then they are less likely to hit you from behind.

Your projects will work better if you consider the pitfalls. That's not being negative, it's just enabling you to be more positive. People who point out these possible problems may well be trying to help. And your relationships could improve if you can say you don't quite understand, but you want to listen, and your support can be relied upon.

If you are a hesitant, inactive, unproductive Two you may well be dissatisfied with yourself. Start to reclaim your potential by looking for the Moon in the early evening sky, when she is four or five days old. See how fresh and shiny she looks. Get up early, touch the dew, go for a walk, have a swim or a jog. Read a page or two of that book you've been meaning to tackle. Make a resolution that you will do certain things, even if you are tired or uncertain. If you get the wheels moving, things will start to become clearer – it doesn't matter if you go wrong or make several false starts.

Associate with people who will give you space, encouragement and jobs to do – or with those who need help. Concentrate ruthlessly on the positive, and be on the lookout for the negative worms that may wriggle in to undermine your efforts. Count your blessings over and over again – even make a list of them to check when sliding downwards. It really is your nature to be positive and active and you owe it to yourself to live this, so imagine each morning that you are taking the brakes off and letting your inborn instincts run free.

COMPATIBILITIES

Twos get on well with Fours and partnerships with Sevens can be pretty hot, though not always easy. Twos and Eights may form an interesting relationship in which the question may be asked, 'Am I a

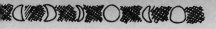

figment of your imagination, or are you a figment of mine?' Fives are likely to indulge Twos and they can sometimes irritate each other. A balanced partnership is possible with a Six.

VISUALISATION

Relax totally, as described in the Introduction. You are at the top of a lush meadow, that slopes gently down towards the east. It is early morning. Dew pearls each blade of grass. It is pleasantly warm in the light of the climbing sun. Insects and butterflies are beginning to stir and far and near the air chimes with birdsong. A gentle breeze comes from the direction of the sunrise, but it is not cold. You smell the wakening scents of earth and flower and feel the vibrancy all around you and through you. Allow yourself to absorb this for a moment. Feel energetic and more alive than ever before. Let the sparkle of the morning enter deep inside you.

As you feel more and more lively, let yourself begin to move. You can run, glide or fly down the slope. At the bottom of the slope there are three huge yew trees, arranged in a triangle. Gently drift into the centre, where it is shadowed. The branches arch above your head like a cathedral and the birdsong peals like bells. You know that you are in a very ancient place. Your feet are now on the ground, and you realise that the tree-roots snake and curl about them. You sit down upon one of them, feeling it is important to rest for a while. You are aware that deep, deep underground, where the roots twist, worms and bugs are busy nourishing the soil.

The sun moves upwards and a shaft of light streams upon your face. Affirm three times, 'I am bright and full of life. Face to the sun, I also respect the darkness and the unknown'.

You see that a girl has come into the grove. She walks towards you. The sun is behind her so you cannot see her face. She carries a gift for you, on a cushion. Can you see what the gift is? Does she speak to you? Take the gift and thank her, even if you are not sure what it is or means. Now you may go out of the copse and move on towards the sunrise, if you wish. Come back to everyday awareness when you are ready and write down what you have experienced.

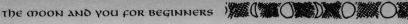

Other Type Twos

Elvis Presley, Paul McCartney, Tchaikovsky, J. R. Tolkien, Clint Eastwood.

Earthly Harmonies

Colours   Oranges, yellows, bright greens and blues.
Oils, flowers, herbs   White sandalwood, fennel, thyme, carnation, orange, peppermint.
Stones   Yellow pearl, blue quartz, topaz, pumice.

TYPE THREE:
REBELS WITH AND
WITHOUT A CAUSE

> *I pushed B-52 and bombed 'em with the blues*
> *with my gear set stubborn on standing.*
> *I broke all the rules strafed my old high school*
> *never once gave a thought to landing.*

Bruce Springsteen, 'Growin Up'

They may come roaring down the road all black leather and screaming steel, or storm controversially into print with a 'Publish and be damned!' Perhaps they are sweating on the squash court or arguing with teacher or boss. Or maybe they are off alone, kicking stones and scowling, while they try to work out why everything seems to be against them. An extreme picture? Of course. But if you cut someone up at a roundabout it might be a Three, so be on the safe side – keep your foot down and your window up!

In the cycle of the Moon, growth is noticeable and established. The pathway has been blazed and by now something should be beginning to be achieved – something that will blossom at Full Moon. There can be a feeling of being able to move mountains, but there can also be a sense of frustration, if things aren't going quite as they should – 'Get going or else!' may be the message. In terms of the Goddess, now is the waning time of the waxing – the first flush of youth is past, and maturity is prepared for. The 'Warrior Goddess' strikes out, climbing, hunting, overcoming. The instincts of Threes are to grapple with challenges, to prove and achieve. They don't feel 'right' unless they are striving, and while this may look unpleasant to more laid back people, for a Three at some level it is 'where they live'. Paradoxically, to be at peace inside, they have to be at war in some fashion, but this state of contention can be immensely creative.

Threes come into the world with something to prove. Life seems to them a concerted effort to catch them with their pants down, and they may behave defensively even when no threat or criticism is dreamed of. Very occasionally some also believe that attack is the best form of defence. These can be verbally aggressive and may even be capable of physical assault. Needless to say it takes a lot more than Moon phase to denote violence. However, if other factors support this, and if they come from a turbulent home, it is possible that Type Threes can be dangerous with their fists.

One Type Three, a double-glazing salesman and rugby player, was every man's mate and every woman's darling. His infectious grin and breezy air made him the office favourite, and if he too readily pushed his foot into people's doorways it served only to make his sales figures rocket. I thought him one of the most good-natured people I had met and was amazed to hear he had a criminal record, and was lucky not to have been 'sent down'. Being curious I just had to ask him about it.

'Some bloke accused me of eyeing up his missus,' he said.

'Were you?' I asked, thinking he probably had.

'Nope,' he said 'But I could see by his eyes he was going to have me, so I got in first and made a good job of it!'

This is an extreme example, and one with which a lot of Type Threes will be unable to identify. None the less every Three has a nose for a fight, whether or not it is unconscious, or with people, things or simply themselves. Somewhere, somehow they want to find trouble before it finds them. Behind this is the symbolism of the Moon's phase. Now she is at her first quarter. The new stage ushered in by Types One and Two is facing its first challenge. There is still the sense of dynamism – in some ways it has increased – but now the fresh concepts have to be re-examined. Are they valid? Will they stand the test of time? Of course, Type Threes don't go around asking themselves this, but they feel challenged deep within. It's as if their insides are the permanent site of a head-on smash.

Threes are not always realistic about opposition. Sometimes they tilt at windmills. Often they will use a sledgehammer to crack a nut, or a pea-shooter against an Exocet. In any case they are courageous and persistent and rarely stay down for long. The most important thing to Threes is to prove things to themselves, but even they do not always realise this. They need to test all beliefs by putting them into practice. They are great troubleshooters and derive satisfaction from correcting other people's mistakes. They can be perfectionists. Often they are their own worst critic, and this is can make them very thorough. They may feel deeply insecure but this is covered usually by their impatient and belligerent attitude. They can see flaws in what they produce that are not apparent to anyone else. Sometimes they can be very hard to please. The approval they find so hard to grant themselves is not lightly bestowed elsewhere.

While Ones and Twos are busy breaking new ground, Threes are often more noted for it. They seem to call attention to themselves by rebelling. Often they like to shock or overwhelm. If they have novel ideas they will get them noticed regardless of the current climate of opinion. Thus, although no more innovative than Ones and Twos they are more frequently in conflict with the Establishment. What the earlier phases have envisioned Threes will fight for. It may seem to them their very identity is at stake, and they have to prove they are someone or they may wake up one day and discover they are no one! Horror! So they may be 'mad, bad and dangerous to know'.

Threes are often noticed as 'strong' personalities. Frequently they are power-houses of energy and can move mountains. Usually they are demanding. Some Threes seem to head-butt their way through life and they can be clumsy, physically or mentally. There are some who feel perpetually hard done by, and these are capable of ceaseless whining. Others really are their own worst enemy, managing to create the trouble they are busy sniffing out.

One Three man, reasonably successful, with a good marriage and family, could not rid himself of the conviction that life had given him a raw deal. He would come home at all hours of the day to catch out his wife in suspected infidelity. Eventually she lost respect for him and did find a lover. Meanwhile finances were a struggle. Hard

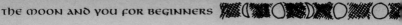

done by again, he couldn't see why he shouldn't 'borrow' something from company funds. After all, didn't he deserve something better? He'd frittered away a cool £30,000 before the accountant – and the law – caught up with him. He blamed it all on his errant wife. The court was sympathetic – Threes can do a wonderful hangdog act – and he got a suspended sentence. Regarding home, wife and daughters he was not so lucky, and is no doubt still shaking his head or kicking himself.

It can be hard for Threes to accept when they are the architects of their own misfortune. After all, there is nothing more ulcer-producing than anger at oneself. Having accepted responsibility – the first hurdle – the next stage for Threes is the kicking oneself routine, and some get stuck at this. Having said this, Threes who have assumed full responsibility for their destiny are tremendously effectual. These are achievers, the high flyers. Dynamic, well-nigh unstoppable, they are not easy to miss. All Threes are capable of this and most attain it at some point in their life, even if they don't retain it.

These people can be found at the top of the tree or on skid row. Some climb ceaselessly while others never haul themselves off their knees for long. Their way seems blocked by something dark and they have vague, lingering guilt feelings. It can be hard for them to see that these obstacles are of their own making. Threes are never content to rest on their laurels, if they have any. They feel they must re-create themselves each day and that they are only as good as the latest day's work. It is hard for them to feel they are good enough as they are. They judge themselves by what they do, and may feel an emptiness within if there are no accomplishments. It is written, 'By their fruits shall ye know them', and many Threes have a string of achievements to their credit but still don't feel they've done enough.

Threes get the most out of life by taking things seriously. They are competitive and play to win. They take the attitude that anyone who says 'It's not winning that matters, it's how you play' must be a loser. Even simple relaxation, such as watching television may set their jaws rigid with concentration. They like to extract as much as possible from everything they do.

Threes have intense vitality except when suffering from one of the ailments induced in them by tension – migraine is a favourite. There is rarely a dull moment with the average Three. One who has his team of wild horses properly under control is really going places. For an eventful life, hitch up your wagon with a Three – and hold on tight!

RELATIONSHIPS

It must be obvious that if a quiet life is your dream then a typical Three is hardly your ideal choice. Because Threes are rarely at peace with themselves they do not easily find harmony with others. Often they are on the lookout for slights, hints that your love is waning, or – threat of threats – signs that there is Someone Else. A Three who has been mishandled in life will be especially hard to relate to, for they will mistrust affection and suspect that they are being manipulated or deceived. Like Nines they can be determined to find the worm in any apple.

On the other hand a relationship with a Three can be exciting in the extreme. Like Sevens they invest a great deal of fantasy in the relationship, but unlike Sevens they are more capable of sustaining it unilaterally. In other words there is not so much to live up to with a Three. If they view you as Kim Basinger or they see Arnie Shwarznegger's torso in your pigeon chest, just lie back and enjoy it. They will happily maintain their viewpoint as they get on with life. Their dreams are uncomplicated, but what they do need from a partner is devotion and endless reassurance. Inside they are very insecure, and anything less than passionate desire will leave them sullen and wounded.

Threes are often very passionate people. They want the best for their partner and the best relationship possible and they are prepared to work hard for this. Relationships are often very dramatic, with lots of slammed doors and emotional 'making up'. Unless there is something lively going on they get the feeling things have died a death. Almost any reaction is better than no reaction. Ignoring a Three can in extreme cases provoke violence. Cool reason may also set a Three gnashing his/her teeth. It may seem sometimes that you

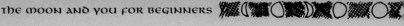

can't win because if you lose your temper and spit out some home truths they are likely to be mortally hurt. Of course what they really want to hear is that you'd die for them, but they probably won't admit that!

As in other areas, Threes feel they have a lot to prove in love. Many doubt their attractiveness and may collect notches on the bedpost to confirm their sex appeal. Because of this they are not always faithful. Of course this is deeply hurtful, but if a Three says it meant nothing this is probably true. It was just an ego trip and what your Three really wants is a few tears and a show of jealousy that will make him/her feel really wanted – for a while. Many people find they cannot sustain such tension and so Threes' relationships may let them down, leaving them even more needy. If the boot is on the other foot and a Three finds him/herself betrayed, expect huge scenes and never to be allowed to forget it.

Many Threes avoid these extremes but do manage to bring to their relationships an intensity and an almost perpetual 'high'. At their best a Three will stop at nothing to prove their devotion, from kissing your feet to sweeping you off them. They do not always remember birthdays or the favourite perfume or aftershave, but they give generously and unpredictably – of themselves as much as anything else.

Threes are fervently sexual and bent on proving their prowess. A Three man may feel he has failed if he only makes love four times on the first night and if his partner doesn't have multiple orgasms. A Three woman may feel disappointed if her man is less than a tiger and blame her spare tyre or any other usually imaginary defect. These ladies do like to feel that they are the most beautiful, sexy creature in town – either that or they are nothing. Because of the tension around all of this, Threes sadly do sometimes experience sexual dysfunction, such as loss of erection or inability to achieve orgasm. A Three who has finally learnt to take everything a little less seriously will enjoy things a lot more. Threes have a sudden sense of humour that can set everyone laughing.

There are unlikely to be many dull moments in life with one of these people. Demanding, moody, sensual, incomprehensible, they can be

very sexy and quite a challenge. If you like to feel you're where the action is, to know you're alive and wide awake, you'll never need to pinch yourself around a Three!

FAMILY LIFE

Threes are especially likely to rebel against parental authority, symbolising as it does the parts of themselves that frustrate them from within. Any opposition feeds their self-doubt, but far from succumbing to it they respond by a determination to overcome. Thus almost any parental instruction can turn into the proverbial red rag to the bull. One might be forgiven for deliberately telling them to do the opposite.

Oppressive parents of Threes need to be aware that their days are numbered. One young man whose father bullied him and was given to beating his mother in front of him one day decided to put up with it no more. At 15 he was the same height as his father. He faced the old man eye to eye and told him he was going to stop – or else! Having successfully defended his mother the teenager felt he had come of age. Unfortunately he proceded to behave similarly, though in a milder fashion, with his own family – a pattern familiar to social workers that certainly doesn't only apply to Threes.

A similar but very tragic tale applies to another young man. Badly abused by a drunken father he eventually floored him in a kitchen brawl. Unable to escape the destructive pattern, however, he killed himself some years later. In case it sounds as if Threes have the monopoly on domestic violence, however, I must stress that this isn't the case. Most Threes wouldn't dream of lifting a finger against their nearest and dearest and are far more likely to expend energy on sport or DIY projects, with which they are rarely satisfied.

The potential of Threes for destruction is there, but like Sevens they are champions of the underdog and often physically brave. One Three man attempted to sort out single-handedly a brawl that ensued during a stag night that he had organised. His success was only partial, but he emerged unscathed.

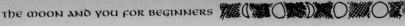

Within four walls Threes do lose their tempers quite readily, but this can be easier to cope with than festering resentment. They prefer to clear the air. They are energetic and prepared to invest in home-making – all the more so because they have a lurking feeling that they might not be doing it very well. Some Threes try to be Superman or woman and it is to their credit that they sometimes come close to succeeding. The bad side of this is that they are often irritable. Threes need to find ways of relaxing in which they can lose themselves.

As parents, Threes feel they must give their children a solid grounding because 'It's tough out there'. Thus they may seem a little harsh. When the school report arrives full of B+ grades, a typical Three parent will ask where the As are. Sometimes they fear that praise will make children 'soft', which is a shame, because Threes love their children fiercely.

Three children are likely to have more than their quota of banged heads and bruised knees. If they are the more sedentary type, tears of frustration over jigsaws and Lego are likely. These children do need constant reassurance that they are acceptable as they are. If they do transgress it should be made crystal clear that it is the action, not the child that is being condemned. A careless rebuke, such as 'You're so selfish/stupid/dirty', will echo down the years in a Three and they may expend futile hours in thankless charity work, obscure study or obsessive showering to prove to themselves that it wasn't true. Three children can be demanding and whining, and as adolescents may be hell on wheels. Try to reassure them they are loved but do not feel you have to supply all they want.

Step-families are mixed blessings to Threes. As stepchildren they can be murder. 'You can't tell me off, you're not my real mum!' is more frequently uttered by a Three than by any other phase. However, step-parents can be stimulating to Threes, and they will love to play games with them, for in some ways the issues will be less strained than with natural parents. As step-parents Threes try hard to do their best, sometimes operating stiffly, from a formula, as a way of coping with feelings. As siblings Threes can be fierce rivals, but they close ranks against outsiders. As absent parents they can be erratic, for the conflicting emotions are hard for them to cope

with. Maintenance and visits may be unreliable, and Threes may be highly critical of the way the custodial parent is raising the children. However, they often try harder in their relationship with their children when they are not living with them, and the arrangement can bring out the best in all concerned.

CAREER

It may be 'tough at the top' but it's a lot tougher at the bottom if you happen to be a Type Three. Their innate competitiveness does not rest easy at the bottom of the pile. They rarely have trouble 'hangin' tough and stayin' hungry', and sometimes they have a touch of unscrupulousness. Mostly this consists of a certain ruthlessness in acceptable wheeling and dealing, but some Threes do cheat a little. If they do this they really are their own worst enemy, for what they mainly cheat is their own sense of satisfaction at what they've done.

Most Threes are exceptionally hard workers and worry ceaselessly about the acceptability of what they have done. Often they will work overtime to perfect it. They like to introduce new systems and get them up and running. They do not always respect tradition and may want to get rid of something (or someone) just because it is old-fashioned, regardless of whether it actually works well or not, and when this happens their disruptiveness is equalled only by their stubbornness. They are great ones for throwing out the silver spoons with the tin cans, and are quite capable of having a row with the boss and slamming the door on job and livelihood in a temper. When the dust settles they begin to tear their hair with worry. Threes are usually very employable, however, and quickly find another niche.

Any career chosen by a Three should give space for their ambition. Whether it is to be the fastest piece-worker, the top salesman or the teacher whose students get the best marks, Threes stretch themselves and others. Whatever the circumstances of their background Threes strive to make the best of themselves, and some rise far above their early family situation. Three is the archetypal self-made man – or woman. They are mostly realistic. 'If the mountain won't come to Muhammed, Muhammed must go to the

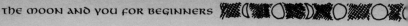

mountain', could be their motto. They don't expect things to come easily, and sometimes they are incapable of believing it when they do. In some ways they are happier when 'up against it' and more than a few Threes have created true misfortune while moaning about imaginary ills.

Threes need to remember that 'All work and no play makes Jack a dull boy'. It can also make him a very sick boy. Threes can be susceptible to tension-related illnesses, from breakdown to heart disease. Sometimes trying to relax just makes them more tense, so they need to find ways of playing hard. Some pastime in which they can lose themselves is essential to a Three, and anything from golf to going to the cinema will do, as long as they find it absorbing.

Female Threes may feel more pressurised than the men, and will try to be perfect housewives, mothers, professional women and lovers all rolled into one. Often they just about succeed, but there may be an ineradicable frown between the perfectly arched brows. They need to remind themselves that their passion for excellence may be unrequited and they could end up gnashing their teeth because they feel they've done nothing properly.

Threes are calculating with their money. They do not like to waste it. However, they do find it hard to bear financial constraints. Lack of money can feel like a personal affront, and spending a form of retaliation. They hate to have to wait for what they want, and they don't like to appear to be penny-pinching – even when they are.

Threes are builders and confronters. They show us the value of perseverance, and that the dust and detritus of demolition are necessary precursors to the building of something new. In many ways they blast the pathways for the innovations presaged by Ones and Twos. This takes courage, but after all, 'Fortune favours the brave'.

MAKING THE BEST OF YOURSELF

At the mere mention of self-improvement I can just see the muscles tense around the neck and shoulders of Type Three – sleeves rolled up to the elbows and let's get on with it! Well, it's not like that. If you're a typical Three, your most pressing need is to learn to relax.

The type of 'relaxation' that involves a lot of lying around is foreign to the instincts of most Threes, so look for some sort of recreation in which you can lose yourself. What you choose to do needs to be totally absorbing, so there isn't room in you for the usual worries and pressures. Your instincts are probably competitive, so complete with yourself to discover the best possible way to 're-create' – anything at all, from hang-gliding to amateur dramatics. And if tension really is a major problem, hypnotherapy can help with this, and aromatheraphy and massage are excellent for dealing with the physical side.

Work to achieve a sense of proportion, and learn to take a deep breath or two before launching yourself into action. Ask yourself some questions. Why am I doing this? What am I trying to prove? Is this something that will really take my life significantly forward, or am I stuck in some old pattern? You will find it easier to relax if you feel sure that your efforts are worthwhile.

If you are a Three who feels perpetually frustrated, then you need to apply your ruthlessness to looking at yourself. Are you gnawing on old grievances? Going over them time and time again really won't help. Are you trying to do the impossible because someone, somewhere along the line gave you the idea that you should? If so, you are unlikely to achieve much, because if something is impossible for you then it is just that – impossible. Write down the impossible demands, the old grievances, burdens 'shoulds' and 'shouldn'ts' on a piece of soluble paper, and flush it down the loo. Watch the water taking it away – whisking the difficulty off with it. Feel the coolness of the water wash over you, internally. Do this every day for as long as it takes to get rid of the unwanted promptings.

COMPATIBILITIES

Two Threes together can be dynamite, and this is also true of Threes and Sevens. Fights are likely with Nines and Eights, and Ones may irritate, as may Fives. Fours may bring some harmony into the lives of Threes, but perhaps the greatest feeling of acceptance may be found with a Six.

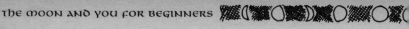

VISUALISATION

Relax totally, as described in the Introduction.

You are in the middle of a vast plain, with the morning sun shining full and bright upon your face. Strangely shaped boulders are scattered all about. Some of them are encrusted with jewels. There are many unfamiliar plants and trees growing far and near. Ahead of you, crowned by the sun lies a high mountain. The slopes are steep. It has a shape somewhat like a pyramid.

You realise that you want to get to the top of the mountain and you set out on your trek, but it seems a very long way. Suddenly you feel yourself lifted off your feet and soaring through the air. Travelling effortlessly you find yourself at the top of the mountain peak. You are aware of a feeling of intense exhilaration as you gaze at the panorama at your feet. Repeat to yourself three times, 'I am effectual. There are no true obstacles in my rightful path.'

You realise that there is a young woman standing next to you. She is athletic and full of energy. In her hand she carries a bow and there is a quiver full of arrows slung on her back. She draws one and shoots it towards the horizon. It soars out of sight. She tells you that the arrow points your way. Looking down you see that the path off the mountain is gentle and smooth – easy to walk.

Now you can follow the arrow if you so wish, or you can postpone the journey. In any case you know that your way is clear and the future holds promise and excitement.

When you are ready come back to everyday awareness, bringing with you a feeling of exhilaration and freedom. If you 'followed' the arrow you may like to write down what you experienced.

Other Type Threes

Alfred Hitchcock, Paul Gauguin, Dylan Thomas, Roger Daltrey, Charles Baudelaire, John F. Kennedy.

Earthly Harmonies

Colours   Bright reds. Sometimes orange. Black, white, dramatic colour contrasts. Blue often has a calming effect.
Oils, flowers, herbs   Ginger, cumin, dragon's blood, wormwood, patchouli, pine, camphor.
Stones   Red pearl, Herkimer diamonds, serpentine, sard, ruby, bloodstone.

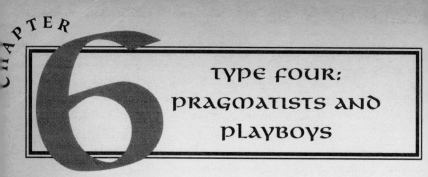

TYPE FOUR: PRAGMATISTS AND PLAYBOYS

When the green woods laugh with the voice of joy
And the dimpling stream runs laughing by
When the air does laugh with our merry wit
And the green hill laughs with the noise of it ...

William Blake, 'Laughing Song'

There are some people for whom everything just seems too easy. Born with a silver spoon in the mouth and a quick quip on the tongue, life is an upwardly mobile glide. Perhaps you can spot them at the centre of an admiring crowd, jumping for joy as their horse wins at the races, or celebrating their latest romantic or business triumph. This is the typical Type Four, for whom life is just a bowl of cherries. Of course they aren't always so lucky. Most Fours do suffer at times, like the rest of us. But if you look closely it is usually possible to spot a particular talent, a unique strength or simply an endlessly supportive friend or spouse. Many Fours who are struggling like to appear like winners and sometimes they convince themselves that's what they are – and that's half the battle.

The Moon has now passed her first quarter, and she is approaching Full. The feeling abroad is that challenges have been surmounted and all is surging towards fulfilment. In many ways this is the most joyful and positive of the phases, filled with pleasant anticipation of life's goodies. This is the 'waxing' time of fullness. We can imagine the Goddess as pregnant, full of the joys of anticipation, blooming, fertile, awaiting the culmination and wonder of birth. The instincts of Fours are to celebrate, enjoy, expand, and they are rarely at ease

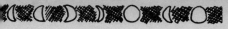

unless they can find a way to do this. Of course birth, whether in the physical sense, of producing a baby, or metaphorically 'birthing' an idea is usually a strenuous and messy process, followed by the burden of responsibility. Fours who also take this aspect on board are able to live the most constructive lives.

Fours are enthusiastic and hopeful. They often refuse to see obstacles, which then obligingly disappear, to the wonderment of sceptics. Sometimes they go to extremes – active, superior and devil-may-care – or simply big-hearted. They have big ideas, liking to feel creative and noteworthy, and they embark on ambitious projects of all sorts, from founding a large centre for healing to organising a clog-dance troup. Even reserved Fours (and there are some) have a certain determination and wilfulness. At their best, Fours have a hearty, infectious laugh and are generous to a fault.

These types believe in living life to the full. They like a joke and are often spontaneously witty, having a store of anecdotes with which to amuse. They are party animals for whom any excuse for a rave-up will do. The noisier ones will love to rock the night away, but they do not offend the neighbours – they invite them along. Everyone is welcomed with an arm about the shoulders and a large drink – Fours are full of natural affection (though they are not above a little hypocrisy at times). Quieter Fours still possess a glow of gladness and can turn a simple glass of wine into a glittering festival. If they prefer Rimsky-Korsakov to rock'n'roll they are none the less affirmers of life at its most vibrant. The quietest Four that I know still admits to 'not being what you'd call a "moderate" person'.

My uncle, in many ways a typical Four, was one of the most charismatic men I have met. He could make magic out of the mundane, and my grandmother was perpetually convulsed by hysterical laughter when he was around. He had many an exotic tale to tell, could play the balalaika, dance like a Cossack, imitate the giants Grumbleguts and Thundertum (whom he had invented), produce exciting gifts at birthdays, and create excursions that he mythologised along the way. My uncle proceded to become a fairly eminent scientist, and a loving and supportive family man – but he never lost the eternal playfulness and *joie de vivre* that were his hallmark.

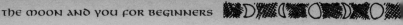

Never be misled into the belief that Fours just don't take life seriously, however. There are some who are guilty of this, the ones who seek to avoid the blood and sweat necessary for delivery, but most are pragmatists. To them life is the 'art of the possible' and often they will be weighing up situations with a lot of cool calculation behind the twinkle in the eye. Usually they have a clear sense of what they want, and if they do not it is of extreme importance to them to determine a goal – they are rarely comfortable just drifting. Less desirably, some Fours may convince themselves that the end justifies the means, if they want something badly. They are opportunists, and they rarely miss an occasion where they can take an advantage – in the nicest possible way, of course. Nor do they like to miss anything interesting that may be happening. In this they resemble Threes. They like to be where the action is and may become a little petulant if they're left out.

Fours do like their own way, and they often succeed in getting it without anyone realising what's happening. Often subtle manipulators, they have a way of making other people think that what they want is really the other person's idea. Most Fours are tactful, but if tact doesn't work they are not above outright demands. There is a healthy self-centredness about Fours, but this can swell to selfishness on occasion.

One young husband – perhaps guilty of the latter – had married his childhood sweetheart, who would do almost anything for him. After a while, as frequently happens, he became bored with the relationship. Not that he wanted to lose his compliant and supportive wife, of course, but he fancied something a bit extra. Surely she would understand – this meant nothing – and after all he wouldn't mind if she did the same. Soon he lighted upon someone who took his fancy, but it was unclear whether the feeling was returned. A merry episode followed where the obliging wife not only drove him to the unsatisfactory assignations (so he could have a glass of wine without fear of the breathaliser), but also gave him advice on seduction. Have you guessed? She had plans of her own regarding someone else.

Things turned messy and sour. Her choice did not meet with his approval as the other man posed too much of a threat and his own

affair refused to blossom. Fours do not adapt well when things fail to go their way and they aren't everyone's darling. Never mind. The erring wife was brought to heel and the unco-operative lover replaced by something more constructive – in this case a degree course in Business Studies. Fours rarely have so little sense of self-preservation as to throw good efforts after bad.

There is a trace of arrogance in some Fours and this can emerge if their sense of specialness is threatened in some way. Their insecurity is hidden even from themselves, but make no mistake, it's there. The drawback is that pride can arouse dislike and disdain, and even provokes aggression from some quarters. The sort of Four who is prone to behave in this way will appear often to be in the centre of some dispute, seeming to be suffering attack and giving the impression of being noble and detached. This is unlikely to be really the case – it takes two to engender conflict, unless the circumstances are exceptional. It is hard to resolve all of this unless the Four in question is prepared to admit to being scared and vulnerable, and to having provoked the trouble at some level.

Fours often appear to be very talented people. I don't think this is because Moon phase indicates special abilities, but if Fours have a gift they develop and exploit it, and they probably don't keep quiet about it. So you will see their paintings, read their poetry and listen to their enthusiastic strummings on their new guitar. There is more than a little of the entertainer in many Fours. One delightful Four lady that I know wrote a romantic novel that was serialised over the tannoy where she worked, and all her colleagues waited with baited breath for the next instalment. Even quieter Fours are not given to false modesty and will display a gentle pride in their achievements.

Usually Fours make life just a little more stimulating for anyone entering their orbit. Some Fours are interested in investigating unusual subjects, such as UFOs or exploring realms of experience such as psychism and mysticism. The urge behind this is the search for fulfilment and the deepening and widening of knowledge, both for themselves and everyone else. They are interested in the useful, which is not necessarily the same as the practical. There is usually an area of special richness to be found in their lives. This might be a

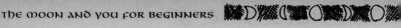

luxuriant garden they have created, a home furnished with that extra bit of taste, or something less concrete such as a group of unconventional friends, or as abstract as a collection of remarkable ideas and theories, which they will put forward with enthusiasm. Fours are broad-minded in the sense that they like to encompass all possibilities.

Fours do like to feel they can cheer people up and that they have the answer to most of the problems that beset us. They are lavish hosts, and if they do go a little over the top on the falling-down-water themselves they are so funny that no one holds it against them. Often they will invest a lot of effort trying to light up the life of a depressed friend. Like Twos they are eternal optimists. Of course this can get a bit much when the budgie's died and the bailiffs are at your door. None the less, Fours who have learnt a little subtlety are marvellously cheering people. They know the power of laughter and are adept at engendering it. There is a true tale of a man who received a cancer diagnosis, giving him only weeks to live. He shut himself away in his room with every funny video he could get and laughed himself crazy for days. To the amazement of the medical profession he cured himself. I have no idea if he was a Four, but he is a good example of the way that the most positive Fours operate.

RELATIONSHIPS

Fours do not readily find happiness in relationships because they are frequently quite fussy. This is not exactly a matter of being pernickety or fault-finding, but they do tend to wonder if there is something out there waiting for them that is better, more exciting, just that bit different, and they don't like to narrow their options. This can make it very hard for them to commit themselves, and some Fours wake up to the fact that their best chances have passed them by. This can give rise to a dramatic depression.

Let me take this opportunity to stress that Fours' good humour is certainly not indestructible and when they do go down it is often in a big way, and they may be unhappy for years. Neither is it only relationships that upset them, but a general dissatisfaction that they

know they are not making the most of things and yet can't quite plug into the positivity gain. Sometimes they can go from one therapist to another in search of the answer (they don't usually suffer in silence) but in the end Fours have to pull themselves up by their own bootstraps and live to fight (and love) another day.

When Fours do fall in love there are rarely half-measures. Their chosen mate is the most beautiful/handsome, clever, talented person imaginable. The eyes of Fours focus on the lovely, and if you never realised what adorable ears you've got it will only take the attentions of a Four to make this very clear.

These are passionate people, usually with a high sex drive. They like to extract the most out of every experience. Often they are noisy lovers, with lots of bedtime giggles and orgasms that wake the neighbourhood. They like a few games and often get a kick out of living dangerously. The idea that they may get caught can add a great deal of spice to their activities.

One teenage girl, a typical Four, was in the habit of slipping her boyfriend upstairs after her parents had gone to bed. After lovemaking rendered all the more delicious by the possibility of discovery, he would creep out by means of the dining room window. One night they miscalculated. Footsteps approached the bedroom when they'd thought all were asleep, and the boyfriend, stark naked, had to leap into the wardrobe to hide. In came the girl's mother, in great distress after a row with her husband. For the following hour her daughter did her utmost to console her, while all manner of private details about her parents' lives (most of which were news to her) were poured out only inches away from the wardrobe door. The fact that the wardrobe kept creaking (it was an antique, and not large) added to the tension. Tearful mother dispatched at last to the sofa, the boyfriend was extracted from his prison. To make matters worse, the four pints of lager drunk earlier had got the better of him and he'd had to relieve himself into one of her Doc Martens.

Most Fours have a tale or two to tell of amorous adventures, from leaps to safety out of bathroom windows, pursued by irate husbands, to exploits in airline toilets. Fours are adventurous, life is for living, love is for giving. These are romantic people, more impressed by a

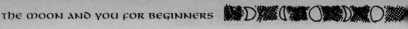

trip by private jet to dinner in Paris than an illicit romp behind the gasworks – and who wouldn't be, you say – especially if you're a Four!

Before you begin to believe that Fours can't be hurt in love, think again. There is something of the big kid in them, and they don't always see drawbacks until too late. Not expecting duplicity (even when capable of it themselves) they are as incredulous and wounded as children when their lover is unfaithful, or lets them down in other ways. Also, having found Mr or Ms Right they pitch in up to the neck, so to speak, and they don't always come up smelling of roses. They may believe that 'love conquers all', as in the case of one woman who took her alcoholic boyfriend home to live with her, airily convinced that she could cure him. Disastrous months followed. She would come home from work to find him sprawled on the bed, floor littered with her books and her CDs and the fridge empty. At night he would prowl the flat, clutching a bottle of vodka and talking to himself. Her job and health suffered, and when she came to her senses getting rid of him wasn't easy. Not to worry. Soon she was back on her feet again, loins girded with fresh resolutions about suitable partners. "But he did have lovely eyes," she still says with a giggle.

In general, Fours do like their mates to be a credit to them. They aren't into looking after lame dogs (unless they're pedigree), and like anyone else, they do like to feel settled. They often have a knack, in the end, of marrying someone conventionally suitable and of benefiting financially or practically from the match. They do not commit themselves in a hurry to something that has little chance of working, although at times in their lives they may seem to be on the brink of just that. There's no warmer, more responsive or more giving partner than a Four who has made their choice for life. Adventures can be undertaken together. What was that song about a 'blanket on the ground?'

FAMILY LIFE

Fours are positive and constructive when it comes to family life. They have a strong sense of family, and like to feel that a close bond exists between all members. They do not like there to be too many rows – they want to see good humour prevail so that everyone can enjoy

themselves together. Outings, parties and get-togethers are valued by them, and are usually great fun, if not hilarious. The typical Four home is a magnet to everyone else. It always seems so pleasant, free and easy, and jolly. Everyone seems to be able to 'do their thing' in the atmosphere of acceptance. Tidiness is rarely insisted upon, but neither does chaos prevail. The home seems well run, and the larder and drinks cabinet are usually well stocked.

However, this may not be as wonderful as it sounds. Fours do love their families but they also strongly need their own space, and if this is not sufficient they can become demanding. Also many Fours like to lord it just a little over the other family members. Usually this takes the form of the spontaneous leadership that is a natural product of a zest for life. However, if something has gone wrong somewhere Fours may resort to getting attention through negative means – persistent 'illness', repeated 'accidents', or disruptive moods. If this happens it needs to be looked at helpfully. All such symptoms need to be interpreted, and some will have their origin in the distant past. It is the life-blood of Fours to feel special in some way, and if this can't find positive expression it is likely to emerge negatively.

It is surprising how many Fours I have encountered who have been neglected or mistreated in some way in their family of origin (as opposed to the family they create as adults). Fours seek to compensate for this in the ways we have looked at, but understandably all such wounds are very hard to heal.

There is a tendency among Fours to have personages in the family amounting almost to gods. Eternally kind, welcoming, generous, uncomplaining and loved by all, the very mention of them seems to bring a glow to the face of the Four who speaks of them. Of course, no one is that good – Fours just like to believe that there is something somewhere totally unspoilt. There is of course, but not on this world, and there are drawbacks to believing one has found it. After all, apparent sainthood can be tyrannous and other worthwhile things can fall into shadow. One young man, a Four in his early twenties, was suffering depression after the death of his perfect grandmother. She had been so wonderful it seemed impossible to get over her loss. It was only when he came to realise her imperfections, one of which

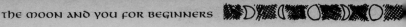

had been her utter determination to hide all her real emotions from his 'crotchety' grandpa, that he was able to be angry with her, and so grieve naturally, as for a real human being. He was also then more able to develop a relationship with his grandfather – a very approachable old man who'd put up with a lot from his paragon of a wife.

As parents Fours are often lavish with their children, and demonstratively affectionate. Their children are a joy to them and they may overcompensate for what their own childhood lacked by giving all they can. Fours' children can be spoilt. Fours need to remember the truism that material things are no substitute for feelings. Not that they are short on feelings, but they always have the urge to do that little bit extra. Fours need also to remember that children need space, and that may include sometimes the right to be miserable. Their children's feelings are not their property and they need to be careful not to become invasive in their wish to make everything okay.

Even more than the adults, Four children need to be the centre of attention. Do not tell them not to show off: encourage them to refine their skills so they can be really entertaining, and encourage them also to be temperate. They need to be brought to realise that they are not only as good as the applause they get, but they have merits deep inside that do not depend on others' opinions. Also, difficult things need to be faced rather than diverted from. It is surprising how many Fours I have encountered who have been the victims of some sort of abuse as children. Parents need to ensure that all the attention these children receive is of a desirable sort.

Step-families can bring out the manic side of Fours, as they compete for first place to try to ensure that everyone is happy. Sometimes they try to win over their ex's spouse. As step-parents they do their best to be as attractive as possible to their stepchildren and they may even try to buy them. Anything that oils the wheels in such circumstances seems fair play to them. As step-siblings they will adapt quite well as long as they can take on a special role of some sort. As stepchildren they can be a handful if they feel resentful, which will be the outcome of feeling ousted. They usually try to get their own way by fair means, but foul cannot be entirely ruled out!

CAREER

Fours are quick to tune into the world and its ways and to do what has to be done to get on. However, they are often dissatisfied with their efforts and may feel they have not done well enough unless they have achieved excellence. The upwardly mobile yuppie may well be a Four.

Fours usually have big ideas. They would rather be a big fish in a small pond than a small one in a lake, but best of all they prefer to be the biggest fish in the biggest lake of all. Of course not all Fours can reach dizzy heights, but their ideas are often on a large scale, if nothing else. Quieter Fours may not exhibit this, but rest assured they have dreams of being prominent in something. Most Fours like to see their name up in lights, even if only in their imagination.

Whatever job they do, Fours need scope for independence and creative thought. Naturally few will be film stars, but they need to be able to put that special 'something' into what they do. Many Fours are natural entertainers. When taking a position Fours need to be sure there is opportunity for advancement. Status is important to them – they need to have the opportunity to shine, and to make original changes. They need to feel they have created something identifiable, whether it is a masterpiece or a new filing system. Their sense of achievement needs to be fed and they will not feel comfortable if they have to work by someone else's plan, regardless of whether it has inspiration or not. They need to put their own stand on what they do, and cannot bear to have anyone breathing down their necks as they work.

Fours like their workplace to be cheerful, and will suffer inwardly if they have to endure tensions. They are the ones who put up the office decorations at Christmas and organise everyone's trip to the pub. When it's their birthday they like a proper celebration and will usually make sure everyone knows about it.

Some Fours imagine that they would be happier running their own business, but they may find the pace hard to sustain. They have flair, but they do need reliable partners. Fours can keep up a steady pace, but drudgery is not for them. They will become moody and faded if called upon to do repetitive, boring or demeaning work.

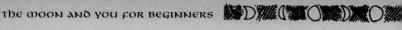

Fours are realistic about money, but this doesn't stop them from being extravagant at times. They tend to feel it is only right for them to have those special shoes, that new CD. They can be resourceful in getting what they need. They hate the thought of poverty and like to have some insurance against this, either literally in the form of an insurance policy, or a nest-egg. Some Fours are lucky with legacies.

These are joyful people. They have an instinctive appreciation of the importance of play in creativity. Their optimism often creates the advantageous conditions they believe in. Theirs is a message of celebration and fruition – that feeling of excitement that comes before the big day that is better than the event itself. Fours need to remember the cliché that 'growth hurts'. Although the thought of heaven on earth is wonderful, attempts to create it in a literal fashion can lead to an unpleasant one-sidedness. Faith in life is another matter, and Fours at their finest can keep that glowing.

MAKING THE BEST OF YOURSELF

There may be the occasional Four who feels this section is unnecessary, because they could hardly be better anyway! Well, you can, and one way to achieve this, if you'll come down off your perch long enough to listen, is to admit you aren't faultless and that you're vulnerable – and that is painful, but most importantly, it is all right. Perhaps you have told yourself you're fine as a defence against criticism, or feel you'll only be lovable if you shine. Really are acceptable, and if you learn to love the imperfect you then it will be all the easier to accept and believe in love from others, as opposed to empty admiration.

In general, Fours do well to remember what we said earlier, about the effort and pain of bringing anything worthwhile into being. The most luscious fruits are at the top of the tree. Climb up to get them – you won't be content with windfalls. You may get bruised and your clothes may tear. There may be less time for enjoyment, but there will be a greater sense of achievement.

If you are a Four who is dogged by frustration, seemingly unable to accomplish much or to find a direction, perhaps you need to realise that there is only one person who can truly help you, and that is

yourself. Naturally that applies to all of us, but there can be a tendency among Fours to hang on to the idea that they're a child of the gods, subject to special favour. There can be a lot of deep sadness and buried anger attached to this outlook, and you may need help to uncover it. However, only you can take that step forward. Like many things, this is easy to say, but hard to do.

Set aside time each day for positive visualisation. Relax and imagine something you would like to be – really imagine it, so that it feels real. Make sure it is something reasonable and possible. The image you create will act as a magnet, drawing you forwards. If this doesn't work then you may need to take a really ruthless look at yourself. Are you secretly angry, resentful, envious?

It is natural to you to celebrate, generate, unfold. Give yourself the space to do this.

COMPATIBILITIES

Fours can make a dynamic partnership with Threes, with whom they are usually able to cope, and things go very well with Twos. With Fives things could feel a bit stagnant, and although harmony is likely with a Six the same could apply. There could be problems with Sevens who have a different sort of intensity, but with Eights the relationship should go well. There are likely to be misunderstandings with Ones and Nines.

VISUALISATION

Relax completely as described in the Introduction.

It is a balmy night, a little before midsummer. A faint glow still lingers in the west, while the Moon, approaching Full, gleams overhead. You decide that you will take a walk. You go out through a garden, heavy with night-time fragrance, and find your steps take you along a country path. The ground is clearly visible in the moonlight and you have a feeling of joyful anticipation.

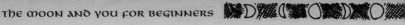

You come round a corner of the path and see spread before you a lake, its still waters pearled by the moonlight. At the bank of the lake a small boat is moored. You walk down to the boat and step in. As it drifts out into the centre of the lake you feel quite safe. In fact you are filled with a sense of the deepest peace. Allow yourself to take in the wonderment of the night sky, the stars and the gleam of the Moon.

As the moonlight beams down upon you it seems to fill you with energy and even more the sense that something important is about to happen – but the boat begins to drift back to land, passing under the shadow of an overhanging willow and getting stuck there.

Out of sight of the Moon you stretch out your hand towards the bank, hidden in inky blackness. You are still confident that something good will happen. Your fingers close around something smooth and firm and the boat begins to move again.

As you emerge once more into the moonlight you can look at what you have picked up. Perhaps it is a jewel, perhaps it is merely a shiny pebble, maybe it is a box containing something special. Whatever it is, it has importance for you, perhaps of a symbolic nature that you do not perceive at first. Say to yourself three times, 'I affirm life, and the greatest joy is often found where I least expect it.'

Come back to the land and walk back to the house. As you pass through the garden you meet a young woman. She is exceptionally beautiful, radiating peace and welcome, and although youthful she is also mature. Discuss your discovery with her if this feels appropriate. Discuss also the reason why your boat got stuck. Afterwards make a note of the answer, however trivial or meaningless it may seem. If not, pass on, benefiting from the warmth of her smile.

Enter the house and come back to everyday awareness when you are ready. Write down anything you feel you would like to remember of your experience.

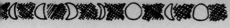

OTHER TYPE FOURS

Chuck Berry, Sophia Loren, Aleister Crowley, Anna Pavlova, Colin Wilson (author notably of *The Occult* and *Mysteries*), Jilly Cooper.

EARTHLY HARMONIES

Colours   All bright colours, rainbow combinations, gold, yellow, orange, rich purple.

Oils, flowers, herbs   Sandalwood, lemon balm, sage, oakmoss, rose.

Stones   Green quartz, aquamarine, lapis lazuli, lepidolite, alexandrite.

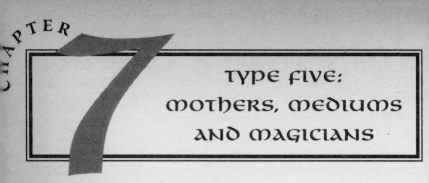

CHAPTER 7

TYPE FIVE:
MOTHERS, MEDIUMS
AND MAGICIANS

The sea is calm tonight
The tide is full, the moon lies fair,
Upon the Straits.

Matthew Arnold, *Dover Beach*

It is hard to imagine anything more magical and unearthly than the light of the Full Moon. Things take on shapes undreamed of in daylight. Myth and enchantment seem far more real than supermarkets and salaries. So people born at the Full Moon must be strange, elf-like creatures – right?

Wrong! It is true that the Full Moon people do have their 'fey' side, but several things need to be born in mind. For one thing it seems that more births take place at the Full Moon than at any other time. This is because of the effect the Moon apparently has on pregnancy and menstruation, as mentioned in Chapter 2. Secondly, although moonlight seems enchanting, in terms of what the Moon signifies this is a time of clarity. In other words Full Moon people are often clearer about their instincts, responses and intuitions, which are the things the Moon signifies. Thirdly, at Full Moon the Sun and Moon are opposite each other. Thus this is a time of balance. Of course, by the same token it may also be a time of frustration, contradiction and 'pulling apart'.

Having said all this, almost every Full Moon person I have known has displayed a psychic gift, to some extent, whether this shows itself in strong but undefined feelings or something more identifiable. The thing about Full Moons is that they are usually unfailingly

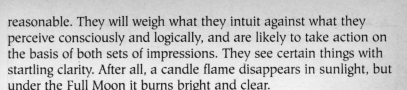

reasonable. They will weigh what they intuit against what they perceive consciously and logically, and are likely to take action on the basis of both sets of impressions. They see certain things with startling clarity. After all, a candle flame disappears in sunlight, but under the Full Moon it burns bright and clear.

In terms of the Moon's cycle, fruition has been reached. This is the time of fullness. The Goddess as Mother presides over her offspring and blesses productivity. Like all mothers she is both protective and detached. To make a child's world manageable a mother needs to empathise – but only so far. She must retain her adult identity so that she is able to teach the child how to cope, and grow. It is the instinct of Full Moon people to enter deeply into experience but also to stand back from it; to nurture – but selectively. They are naturally drawn to rapport and tenderness. Equally, their instincts tell them to remain detached. They need to honour both impulses in order to feel inwardly comfortable.

One Full Moon man had been informed by mediums on several occasions that he was extremely psychic. This was confirmed by his experiences with the ouija board. The slightest touch of his finger sent the glass flying from letter to letter. Sometimes it moved even before he touched it.

Fascinating and amusing conversations commenced with 'spirit guides' from Atlantis and Ancient Egypt. After a few evenings spent doing this, poltergeist activity began. Loud banging resounded around the walls. When the noise was closest to my friend he said 'Boo!' Silence! Things never seemed out of hand because he remained so level-headed, and that is not easy to do when hairbrushes and glasses of water take on a life of their own. He went on to complete an Honours degree in philosophy, and few subjects require more logic than that.

If there are so many Full Moon people, one might expect this to be reflected in what is generally accepted as çharacteristic of the majority, but this is only true to a very limited extent. Full Moon people are not so numerous as to make that great a difference, and the concentration of births seems to include types Four and Six. What I have noticed, however, is that Full Moons seem more often than not to adopt the emotional climate of their times. They react as the majority would. For instance, to the more quixotic there can be a grimly amusing side to news items reporting tragedies, reflecting as they often do someone's unbelievable foolishness. A sarcastic laugh from a Full Moon would, however, be comparatively rare, although they might well make some cool observations. One should not assume from this that the Full Moons are never innovative – they are. Usually however, this will be with regard for harmony and with sympathy for opposing views.

Full Moons are often creatures of habit. This is not so much a rigid routine but more a sense of rhythm, ebb and flow and 'rightness'. 'There is a tide in the affairs of men ...' wrote Shakespeare – and indeed one of his traditionally quoted birthdates (no one can be sure about this) makes him a Full Moon. These types are aware that there is a time and a place for everything, that opportunities have to be seized when they are present but that generally one should go steadily about one's business. They like to feel that 'God's in his Heaven and all's right with the world.' Part of this 'rightness' means that one has a sensible bedtime, and never goes on holiday without a toothbrush. One Full Moon Doctor of Psychology never leaves home without his teapot and special blend of Assam!

It is important for Full Moons to feel secure and to be surrounded by their familiar things. They like the knowledge that the next pay cheque will arrive on schedule, and they like to see things of beauty in their environment. These might be special pictures or ornaments, or a collection of plants. They appreciate peace and a sense of unobtrusive abundance. They like to have something to take care of, and many are fond of animals, such as cats, although they are unlikely to appreciate dirt. Unless Virgo is strong they are not specifically neat, but they can find mess unaesthetic. They need to feel their lives are creative in some way.

Security must not mean stagnation, however. Full Moons have an urge to keep moving, for they sense that it is rarely possible to stand still in any sphere, and lack of forward motion can mean slipping backwards. They like to keep their life path under review, looking to discard the outworn, thinking about what they should have learnt or

be learning, and trying to make improvements. Many are earnest students of themselves, striving for honesty, bouncing back and forth from logic to intuition like a perfectly controlled tennis ball. Any conclusions have to be reasonable but also imaginatively stimulating. They can be quite tough on themselves because they do not believe in avoidance. However, it is rare for them to talk about their self-analysis. They are often strong on common sense and may also fear that self-indulgence may lead to imbalance. They put boundaries around themselves because they are all too aware of the boundlessness at their core. If they say, 'A place for everything and everything in its place,' that is because that is safest.

Those born when the Moon is Full prize calmness. They feel threatened when ruffled or disturbed. Because of this they can give the impression that they are bland, and almost unreachable – it is hard to know what is going on under the surface. They can seem maddeningly detached and one can be forgiven for believing they either don't care or are too shallow and empty to feel very much. This is a big mistake. Still waters run deep, and there is plenty lying 'full fathom five'. Whether it is pirate's gold or a hungry octopus can be dangerous to discover!

Full Moons have much to offer in the way of encouragement and support if one can appreciate their ways. They do love to feel productive, and some are very protective to the less strong. There is a 'motherliness' about even the males, and if a 'there, there' accompanied by a pat on the head doesn't feel like the last word in empathy, at least it is kind. Sometimes dredging the depths is of doubtful value – certainly to Full Moons. Often they can imbue companions with the conviction that there is an answer to everything, and order can and will be achieved. Sometimes they even make one feel guilty and unbalanced – it seems foolish to admit one's inner conflicts in the face of their Mona Lisa inscrutability. And yet there can be something hypnotic in that gaze that somehow lures out the unspeakable, like a python mesmerised by a snake-charmer.

If the foregoing makes Full Moons sound a little unexciting, think again. A Full Moon out of control is not a pretty sight and they know it. Their potential excesses of self-pity, irrational anger,

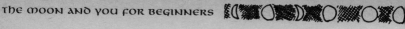

violence and passion are truly scary – most of all to themselves. After all, Full Moon is the time of madness. If Full Moons prefer to avoid turbulence that is because they know the dangers – and most werewolves would agree!

RELATIONSHIPS

Full Moons are not solitary types. In many ways it is in relationships that they find themselves. Partners teach them a great deal about themselves, and they need someone to communicate with, and to discuss all the things they are reflecting upon. They bring to partnerships much strong feeling and commitment, and in general they like to be 'up front' although they may value this more in their partners than themselves. A Full Moon who is disappointed by her/his current relationship is quite capable of deceit and may well rationalise this so thoroughly that they avoid feeling guilty – almost!

These people expect things from a partner. Their demands are rarely excessive, but they are usually quite clear about what they want and are unlikely to put up with less. For instance they expect fairness. Generally prepared to keep their side of any bargain, they will not tolerate a partner falling short without good reason. They like issues to be clear, and if they do not get commitment from a partner they will want at least to know exactly where they stand. They dislike ambivalence but can often find themselves torn two ways. They like to feel they are cherished and will return this by being reliable and caring, but if they feel short-changed their selfish side will surface. Certainly they feather their own nest, but they reason that that is only common sense. They see the pitfalls in too much dependency.

Full Moons usually have quite a strong sex drive. They see sex as a true expression of love and a healthy way to expend energy – of which Full Moons have a good supply, except for off days. They are not especially interested in anything kinky, and while quality is certainly more important than quantity, they often want the latter. They are gentle lovers and greatly appreciate all forms of loving response. Comfort is important to them – if it's going to be the back seat of a car it had better be a Bentley. They are also surprisingly

private people. 'Why don't we do it in the road?' is likely to get a very short answer. Having said this, they do readily see that sex is fun.

There is a certain type of Full Moon who is quite cynical about sex. They may advocate free love and bounce from partner to partner like a party balloon – and with about as much substance. They may react with disdainful surprise if accused of coldness. How uncivilised! How demanding! Don't you know we are all free spirits? This type is in flight from deeper feelings and until they can come to terms with them they can be very hurtful and best avoided if you want more than a fling.

On the occasions when indecision afflicts Full Moons it is a pretty thorough division and they may go on agonising for a long time, lamenting the fact that they can't seem to get both sets of attributes in one partner. To be torn between two lovers is all too common for Full Moons. Adventures of this type may go on for years, as Full Moons often retain their good looks and energy well into mid-life. One attractive Full Moon lady of fifty, still besieged by admirers, has agreed to live with Jack, for the security and comfort he offers, but however hard she tries to convince herself to the contrary, every so often she has to admit it – he is boring! Not only that, he doesn't share her interests, and that is important to Full Moons. So, enter Jim – once more. Lively, generous and with at least a passing interest in her pursuits, a weekend away with him is irresistible. For a while, free from the Sunday-roast-followed-by-a-sleep routine, she has a great time. But doesn't he go on! So back to good old Jack, who at least gives her some peace, wishing and wishing that she could find some magic to combine the best of both.

Sometimes it seems that these types are quite calculating about their love life. One young Full Moon woman, having lived with a man considerably older than herself for some years, began to wonder about the green grass on the other side. On holiday she met a wild Irishman who swept her off her feet. His broad shoulders and lopsided grin would, it seemed, whisk her off to the coast of Connemara. She talked of little else and I assumed she was packing her bags – but no. She expected a letter, and when that came replied, and looked for another. 'What are you waiting for?' I asked

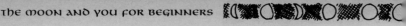

her. 'To see if he loves my socks off,' she answered. Socks still in place, she married her long-term partner the following year, and is quite content.

Another attractive Full Moon told me quite candidly that emotional excesses could not go on indefinitely, and that love-lorn obsession was a blind alley. She resolved her dilemmas by self-possessedly running four relationships at once. It is a tribute to her *savoir-faire* that none of the men ever found out that he was not her only lover. As far as I'm aware she is still going strong with all four to this day.

In case Full Moons sound too much like cool cucumbers I must let it be known that they are capable of immense passion, and sometimes it can drive them to extremes, as with one Full Moon who dragged his faithless wife across the room by her hair. Full Moons are often quite terrified at the thought of this sort of lack of control, and will be very careful where they give their heart, especially when 'once bitten'.

If you are where a Full Moon has, in Othello's words, 'garnered up' his or her heart, this is something to be treasured, and perhaps even feared. Only a Type Nine can brood like a Full Moon, and that calm veneer may be only skin deep.

FAMILY LIFE

Full Moons often come into their own in family life for this seems the perfect sphere for the showing of reasonable sentiment. They can regulate the lives of their loved ones and work towards harmony for all the family. In fact they can live their feelings without having to overemphasise them. Many Full Moons make dedicated parents, but I have also known a good proportion of them with no children, or perhaps only one. In that case they will often turn their nurturing onto the partner.

Full Moon men will usually readily rattle the pans and rustle up a meal, clearing up the kitchen thoroughly afterwards. When called upon to act as house-husband they do so with efficiency, and I have known more than one Full Moon man take on a virtually full-time domestic role while his wife acted as breadwinner. This has less to

do with views about equality of the sexes than with a simple liking for domesticity. There is nothing stick-in-the-mud about this. To a Full Moon, home is a castle, and the habits and routines it enshrines are the very fabric of society.

Of course hearth and home are the strongholds of feminine power, and Full Moons of both sexes usually have a healthy respect for this. They know that 'The hand that rocks the cradle rules the world.' Very few Full Moon men kid themselves for one moment that women are the weaker or inferior sex. At their best they have a sincere appreciation of the feminine in all its aspects; at their worst they may seek to compete or emulate – and that can be hilarious! After all, not everyone is a Keith Floyd in an apron!

Full Moons regard parenthood as a fulfilling function. They are usually good at keeping their children organised and will remind them about social commitments, homework and to 'eat an apple a day'. They regard it as very important to be reliable parents. Sometimes, however, they may be a little simplistic in their approach. After all, humans are not little birds. They need more than food, warmth and the comfort of the nest until ready to fly. A child coming home on a winter's day may love the tea and crumpets provided by Full Moon Mum, but may sometimes have a greater need to talk about why Jane isn't speaking to her, or why he hasn't been picked for the football team. It's not that Full Moons don't care, but they may need to remind themselves that some situations demand more from them than 'Poor darling, eat your tea,' and that they have to risk being 'dragged in' emotionally. By the same token, these parents often find the rebellious teen years especially difficult.

Children born at the Full Moon may be very sensitive, and they will be especially upset if they feel rejected by their peers. It may be hard for them to adjust if they have to move house or school, and they are not often happy playing on their own. Their tears, however, are soon dried, unless there is something seriously wrong. This needs to be watched. A severely bruised Full Moon may go into his shell for a long time. These children are very imaginative and will sometimes have playmates that only they can see. Needless to say, they should never be mocked or talked out of what they sense.

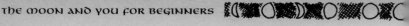

Creative pursuits such as drawing or music should be encouraged if there is any sign of aptitude.

Step-families hardly conform to the Full Moon ideal of family life, and they can be secretly jealous of ex-partner's new relationship, of stepchildren and step-siblings. However, they will strive to preserve equilibrium, and go through the right motions, if nothing else. Sometimes they can be manipulative. They do not readily forget emotional hurts – but neither, for that matter are they likely to forget birthdays and anniversaries. Full Moons can have memories like elephants, which may or may not be an advantage. In an argument a Full Moon can confront you with misdemeanours from years back, quoting day and hour with an accuracy you could not hope to challenge.

Finally we must emphasise the importance of Mother to these folk. Usually she is respected – almost venerated. Sometimes she is deeply resented (no one remembers childhood neglect better than a Full Moon), and sometimes imitated or competed with. The image of her that each Full Moon holds within is an important force in their life.

CAREER

Creativity is important to these people and this needs to be expressed in their work. Some will be artistic, and then what they have produced is clearly identifiable. But even a Full Moon who works in a bank or insurance office will like to feel he or she has composed something, and if it isn't a symphony a set of crucial figures will do. The key here is appreciation. Full Moons like to be seen to be worthwhile. If their boss never says 'Well done,' they become more and more faded. It is not enough to have some standing in respect of other employees. They will complain, withdraw, and eventually leave.

The thought of falling down on one's commitments is frightening to anyone, but to Full Moons it is especially scary. If unemployed they worry ceaselessly, and will make themselves quite ill going on and on about what they must do, but often not quite dynamic enough to

do what is necessary. If they feel they have failed or been rejected it will be a case of 'My get up and go got up and went.' However, for the lucky few who are untroubled by a mortgage or who have private means, time at home is welcomed. Full Moons take very well to being at home, and enjoy working from home.

Full Moons have a sense of dignity and pride and they feel that organising is better than agonising. Although appreciation is vital, it is equally important for them to meet their own high standards. All things being equal, these are reliable people who will hold down a nine-to-five job and work hard. They like to be on good terms with their colleagues. They are usually philosophical about office politics and will seek to pour oil on troubled waters – as long as they are not involved. On the odd occasion when outrage overtakes them they can be impossible to pacify and take a long time to forgive. As for forgetting – forget it!

The pay-packet is a tangible sign of appreciation. Full Moons are quite aware that man does not live by praise alone and will become cynical about a boss who doesn't put his money where his plaudits are. They prefer to have a company pension and health scheme set in place. Full Moons are generally well organised about money, balancing incomings and outgoings and preferring to have a nest-egg. Mostly they are generous, looking for their reward in a smile of appreciation. If it is not forthcoming they can be deeply hurt, and will certainly think twice about future spending.

Full Moons are bringers to fruition, but they are also creatures of contrast. They show us all the value of balance, that there are two sides to most things and that both logic and inspiration are essential. There are many splits in our general view of life – good/bad, male/female, spirit/matter. Full Moons can play a part in healing this.

MAKING THE BEST OF YOURSELF

Although internal balance is very important to you, and you prize intuition as well as reasoning, you do sometimes find this equilibrium hard to maintain, and the chances are the scales tip on

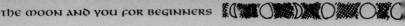
the side of logic. This is hardly surprising. Logic is something that is respected – in fact exalted – in our culture, whereas intuition is regarded with suspicion.

You need to reclaim your intuitive side, because without it you are lame. You can do this in many ways. Maybe you could try Tarot, not for the sake of fortune-telling but because the beauty of the symbols is stimulating to the imagination. You could also find astrology, palmistry and graphology interesting, for these subjects also have a logical side.

Take note of your dreams, for these are very important clues to the workings of the unconscious. They are also a fascinating and colourful testimony of your inner life, which, like the hidden part of an iceberg, is far larger than what shows.

Make sure that you expose yourself to the light of the Full Moon when you can, for it can release energies you never knew you possessed. One Full Moon man I knew practised meditation for hours under the Full Moon and felt absolutely brimming with energy and ideas the following day – despite lack of sleep.

Whatever you do you may still hear a cynical voice whispering 'Phooey!' Well, let it. It needs to be heard. It will only get louder if you try to muffle it – but don't let it stop you.

If you are a Full Moon immobilised by indecision, rather like the poor donkey in the story – dying of hunger because he couldn't make up his mind between two equidistant bales of hay – then you too may benefit from the above advice. Stagnation could result in your spiritual starvation. It really does not matter if you are wrong – indeed that is a prerequisite for learning. Hold your nose, and jump in. The road to success is paved with mistakes that became the building blocks of achievement.

It is your instinct to produce, so do so. Even if you have to tear it all down and start again, what you have learnt will stay intact.

COMPATIBILITIES

Ones and Nines can be good with Full Moons as they challenge them to face things they might prefer to ignore. Threes and Sevens

may irritate. Fives will indulge Twos and Eights. Things could be a bit stagnant with Fours and Sixes.

VISUALISATION

Relax yourself totally, as described in the Introduction.

You are in an orchard-garden, heavy with the scents of many flowers and fruits. Here the season does not matter. There are roses, jasmine and gardenia. Apples, strawberries, peaches are all ripe and abundant. It is midday, warm and slightly misty. The sunlight is gentle, the shadows cool. The air is still, and beneath your feet the grass forms a lush carpet. Allow yourself to absorb the deep peace and abundance of this place.

Ahead you see a particularly beautiful tree. Its branches arch gracefully, laden with ripe fruit. You walk towards the tree, feeling the soft grass underfoot. Beneath the tree waits a woman. She is neither young nor old, but she is beautiful. Her unbound hair hangs below her waist, her face is calm. She smiles and points towards a pool beside the tree.

As you approach the pool you see that its surface is inky-black. You are aware that it is very deep. It does not seem to be reflecting the branches of the tree that overhang it. The Lady tells you to approach it, because it is the source of all the fertility in the garden. As you look down into it, you see that your face is reflected back at you, but there are no other reflections. The Lady tells you there is nothing to worry about, and asks you what you see. You may describe your face to her, and any other things that occur to you. Then stand up and affirm 'I am peaceful, balanced and all parts of me are beautiful and acceptable.' Say this three times.

You may stay and explore the garden if you wish. When you are ready, come back to everyday awareness, bringing with you a feeling of peace and acceptance. Write down anything you might like to remember of what you have experienced.

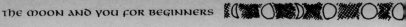

Other Type Fives

Goethe, Shakespeare, Michael Jackson, Edith Piaf, Cliff Richard, Marc Bolan, Rupert Brooke, James Joyce.

Earthly harmonies

Colours   White, cream, silver, most light or bright colours, yellow sometimes. Soft pale blues and greens. Sometimes a full 'royal' purple.

Oils, flowers, herbs   Gardenia, jasmine, coconut, lotus, mistletoe, copal.

Stones   Moonstone, crystal (i.e. clear quartz), opal, kunzite, spinel, carnelian.

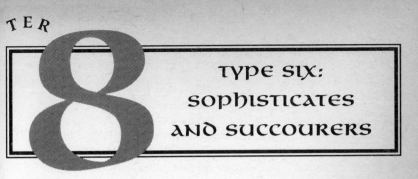

TYPE SIX:
SOPHISTICATES
AND SUCCOURERS

How sweet the moonlight sleeps upon this bank!
... soft stillness and the night
Become the touches of sweet harmony.

Shakespeare, *The Merchant of Venice*

Whether you have been crossed in love or have woken up to find that the slugs have eaten your best lettuce plants, Type Six are the ones to call on for help. Always ready with soft words for sore hearts and arnica for bruised knees, these people are a magnet to the needy. Sometimes they are veritable St Francises, surrounded by convalescing cats and birds with broken wings.

At this stage of the Moon's cycle she is just past Full – this is the 'waning' of fullness. The Goddess, as Mother, realises that her children are growing and the time is approaching when she will be turning her attention elsewhere. Her care is general, rather than particular. The time of fruition, balance and completion is just beginning to fade. There is a sense of reduction in energy, of ebb. Thoughts turn inwards, towards meanings, rather than outwards, towards action. This does not mean that the final four types are inactive (although with the possible exception of Type Seven they can occasionally be lazy). However, when actions are closely examined they seem to relate more to place in society rather than the establishment of identity.

This increased sense of detachment begins to appear in Sixes, with their languid, *laissez-faire* attitude. It is their instinct to heal and help, but when true to themselves they also realise the need to be able to let go. They feel at home taking care of things, but they must not be tied to a slavish or restrictive role. Their inner harmony depends on freedom to take care in an inclusive way, and to be free to tend the 'garden of their soul'.

Sixes are great acceptors. They can be extremely easy-going, and sterner friends may tell them that they let themselves be dumped on (as they leave their children to be minded or their hems to be stitched). However, Sixes really do love to be wanted. Life is worthwhile to them if they feel they can lend a helping hand. They do not always need profuse thanks. Often it is enough to them to know that they have accomplished something worthwhile. However, before it seems they're up for canonisation, what they are really doing is feeding their very human need to be needed. Their egos are as active as anyone else's and they are gratified by knowing they have done some good.

These people often have a languorous air, but if the harmony of their life is disrupted or they are feeling insecure they will be deeply agitated. However, this is unlikely to be obvious. In most circumstances they will appear laid back, and their movements are usually graceful and co-ordinated. If anyone can bite their nails stylishly, it's a Type Six!

Sixes can be true lounge lizards. Usually they are relaxed in company. They like to entertain and to dress elegantly. Loyal to their friends, it gives them pleasure to see people at their ease. Even more outward bound Sixes display a certain urbanity and bonhomie. Whether it's an expedition to the Matterhorn or a picnic in the park, Sixes will like to see it run smoothly, and with attention to comfort. Sixes are usually diplomatic and quietly wise about human nature. A Type Six hostess would never make the mistake of sitting the Methodist spinster from next door at the side of the struggling gay artist she had just befriended – unless of course she knew they shared a passion for Animal Rights! Any such common denominator would be cleverly spotted and exploited by most Sixes. The tragedy of Romeo and Juliet would never have taken place if the Capulets and Montagues had been surrounded by Sixes.

Sixes like to enjoy themselves. They can be prone to self-indulgence. Often they enjoy a little limelight, but will rarely hog it. Their smooth

way of expressing themselves often commands an audience, and there can be something hypnotically soothing about them. Preferring balance and harmony, they will do what they can to restore it, if it is disrupted. Usually they have a strong sense of their own dignity. Some Sixes develop a glossy persona and they can be extremely uncomfortable if this becomes in any way cracked or strained. They do not like others to see them at a disadvantage. Like Fours, they do like to feel just a little superior, and if they betray the fact they're not totally 'above that sort of thing' they don't know where to put their faces.

Many a village fete is built on the industry of Sixes, giving their time and their jumble, and entering their champion turnips for the gardening competition (many Sixes have 'green fingers'). There is a bit of a 'do-gooding' streak in Sixes and they like to be seen as pillars of whatever society they inhabit. Playing 'lady bountiful' is just up their street. Believing that 'it is more blessed to give than to receive' they may forget that gratitude is a form of giving also. Buying a present for a Six may be a thankless task – not literally, for they will express thanks profusely. However, they will find a way to repay the gift twofold rather than feel they have been outdone in generosity.

Sixes are not always completely sincere. Liking to preserve harmony and to be indestructibly pleasant, they will hide their feelings under a bland veneer – most of the time! One delightful elderly gentleman, living on his own, always welcomed us as children. He was the 'good shepherd' of the neighbourhood, shopping for the sick and gardening for the lazy. Of course he was eternally besieged by the needy of all shapes and sizes. Sitting at his window he would watch them coming down the path, nodding and waving, the picture of welcoming benevolence. As we grew older we realised that he was muttering the most fearful curses at his visitors, through his smiling teeth! He was just incapable of saying 'no'.

Do-gooding can be a power trip for Sixes. Their endless giving can make others feel guilty, beholden or inferior, and they can sometimes feed off the misfortune of others – for many Sixes wouldn't know what to do in a world where everyone was happy.

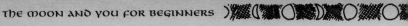

Perhaps they would feel useless and unwanted, and that would be dreadful!

Not only do Sixes often conceal their discordant emotions in the interest of harmony – they may also repress them completely. This can in the end lead to greater problems. One Six man, married to his childhood sweetheart, found that he was having disturbing dreams of violent attack. Things worsened. Soon he was afraid to go in lifts and dreaded driving his car. When at the bank where he worked he began to feel that the others were eyeing him darkly. At Christmas, at home with his family, he found himself haunted by the fantasy of stabbing his wife with the knife she had used to cut the turkey. Seriously alarmed he sought therapy, and after many months came to realise his savage anger at his wife for the way she managed to dominate him through being 'unwell'. No longer afraid of watching eyes, he now had to face the pain and confrontation of divorce – something he'd been fleeing from. Sixes like to keep their own counsel, as silence can be a position of power. However, some things are better said.

Sixes are not always as self-assured as they appear. They are niggled by self-doubts that can push them to ever-greater extremes of do-gooding. Occasionally a stubborn or demanding streak emerges, and when it does there may be no doing anything with them. They need periods of quiet when they can enjoy music. Often they are resourceful, and may do beautiful embroidery or woodwork, or make delicious cakes. Deeply kind, their power to be of benefit to others is their life-blood. The world turns all the smoother for the Sixes oiling the wheels.

RELATIONSHIPS

As you might expect, Sixes' love of harmony is reflected in their relationships. Companionship and common ideals are valuable to them. They enjoy shared excursions and cosy fireside chats, and they are happy with a division of labour, as long as it is a fair one. Secretly, however, they won't struggle all that hard if someone else is willing and able to take responsibility for unpleasant chores. Sixes

enjoy caring for their partners – although they may have to compete with distressed friends, stray dogs and starving hedgehogs!

Sixes are wise about human nature, but I have known several who didn't carry this common sense into their relationships. It's not that they expect their partner to embody a fairytale prince or princess, but Sixes do have a somewhat dreamy side. They can be 'away with the fairies' when it comes to deciding what they can realistically live with. Sometimes they can be quite clear about what a partner is like, and what they are like themselves, and yet still not perceive that they are incompatible, even when it's as plain as the nose on your face to all their friends. In this way a Six who loves ballet and opera may find him/herself hitched to someone obsessed with football – and incompatibilities can go far deeper than that. It's not that Sixes are necessarily swept away by passion. They just feel they can pour the honey of their tolerance over all the brittle bits, and wave an airy-fairy hand at anyone who disagrees. 'Oh, it'll be fine,' they say – but sometimes it isn't.

These people are romantic. They like to be treated as if they are special, and they like to feel the relationship has pride of place. If you're married to a Six, please don't think about watching the wrestling or dishing the dirt for hours on the phone with a friend if it happens to be your anniversary! Such insensitivity will stretch the patience of a Six to the limit. And don't presume on an established relationship to the extent of leaving dirty undies in the bathroom. Sixes are refined. They see no reason why good behaviour should not endure, and aesthetics are usually in the back of their minds – so false teeth stay in, for goodness sake!

Sexually, Sixes are gentle and open-minded. These are worldly people, often quite hard to shock. They will be willing to try most things to please their mate, and can be resourceful and imaginative in bed. Often they are past-masters of seduction, whatever their appearance. They seem to know instinctively how to arouse and how to satisfy. In general they are loyal. They are unlikely to get very upset about a bit of flirtation on the part of their partner as long as it doesn't go too far. In their youth, Sixes can sometimes be almost promiscuous, but they are just as likely to remain dreaming

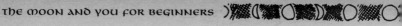

on the sidelines. There is a small part of them that may think, 'Oh, what does it all matter,' and not bother to get involved. They often prefer the other party to make the advances.

Sixes may sound rather ideal mates and in many respects this is true – because Sixes want so much to be perfect. The drawback is that a lot may get shoved underneath the carpet in the name of overt harmony, to the extent that somebody trips over it in the end. Sixes can be forced to admit, after a long time spent ironing out all the wrinkles, that their relationship is a bit bloodless and they really would like more. This is sometimes solved by a civilised affair that Sixes convince themselves isn't really being unfaithful. Sometimes things get more crucial, however.

One woman, having hypnotised herself into believing that her fifteen-year marriage was perfect was 'knocked for six' (to coin a phrase) when the attractive tutor at her evening classes made a pass at her. Having repudiated him clumsily (Sixes' urbanity is not indestructible), her emotions were in a whirl. She found herself writing him a confused, passionate letter. Bewildered, her admirer backed off. There ensued a complex little episode in which no one quite knew what was happening – and then her husband found out. Feeling utterly foolish the woman denied anything important had happened – which it hadn't in a way – and resumed life somewhat chastened and wiser about herself, but with several issues left to be resolved.

If Sixes can learn to be as open-minded and tolerant of their own less acceptable side as they are of others they will indeed be likely to enjoy the perpetual harmony they long for.

family life

It is obvious by now that Sixes prize peace, and they will go a long way to preserve this in their family life. Some even opt for a single life rather than put up with the chaos of a typical family. Sixes may be tolerant of the foibles of general humanity while finding them more difficult to endure close to home.

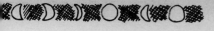

There is a side to some Six people that likes to be in control. Only by holding the reins firmly do these types feel they can maintain equilibrium. Perhaps this is not quite peace at any price, but it can certainly be peace at the price of self-expression and sincerity – and not only on the part of the Sixes themselves. This type of Six can be heard uttering, 'Now, now, that will do,' with steam-rolling finality. Many Sixes are also capable of the sort of statement that runs: 'We just aren't jealous/angry/competitive – we're just not that sort of family.' In this way Sixes really can rule their families with an iron hand in a velvet glove – and display a little snobbery, too!

Sixes are great ones for propagating family myths such as 'The Browns have always been intelligent – just naturally clever, you know.' Mrs Brown's youngest has just failed all her GCSEs and the eldest barely holds down a job as a window-cleaner in between benders – which are the only occasions when he discovers how disreputable he can be. The rest of the time he believes his mother's propaganda, which is that he possesses utter brilliance that will out eventually. None the less, the family harmony is cemented by the belief that they all know a thing or two that no one else does.

Since these people are so naturally accommodating and charming, it is easy to miss the grain of pure granite in them. When pushed they can be quite unbelievably stubborn. This, coupled with their dislike of discord, can give rise to ridiculous situations where members of the same family refuse to speak to each other – as in 'Peter, will you ask your father to pass me the sugar, please?' One Six lady, living near her sister in a small village, did not speak to her for two years. When accosted by her sister outside the local post office, she asserted there was nothing wrong. Things having patched themselves up, she is all smiles and arms full of home-grown vegetables for this sister. On the surface all is well, but the underlying problem can hardly be said to have been aired.

Sixes make generous and affectionate parents, who will do anything for their children. Birthday parties and Christmas get-togethers are impeccably conducted, with an eye on making an impression. Often Sixes will struggle considerably to ensure their children have all they need for their amusement and education, even finding school fees they can ill afford. In return, however, they do like to see family tradition preserved. A Six father who owns a business or farm will love to pass this on to his son. Sixes are not demanding parents, but the unspoken weight of their expectations – even if it is only for the child to be happy and 'normal' – can be a load to bear. Six parents try so hard to be understanding and are puzzled when their adolescent children still rebel – because that is often what adolescents need to do, regardless.

As children, Sixes are usually helpful. They like to set the table or weed the garden – generally they like to feel part of adult activity, whatever it may be. Usually they like to keep pets, and they get a kick out of helping mates do homework. Often they are quite precocious and will be well aware of what's going on among the adults. If there is strife they will feel deeply anxious and will try to heal the rift. As children they are quite conscious about keeping up with the Joneses and so they can be expensive to indulgent parents. They do like to have a nice room in which to entertain their friends and show off their possessions.

Sixes who are part of step-families like to feel that everyone is getting along. They may like to show that they can cope with such life events smoothly, and all in the best possible taste. After all, there is no point in being uncivilised. They may try to befriend their ex's spouse and will be philosophical about any trouble from that quarter. Children of divorced parents will stay loyal to both and may try to bring them together. With step-parents they look on the bright side. Providing their day-to-day life is not unduly disrupted they settle reasonably well into step-families, although they may be upset – as everyone is – at the breaking up of the domestic bliss. They will try to console their parents and even attempt to advise. Once a new relationship is actually in place they will do their best to maintain it. A Six child will often 'be strong for Mummy' and in so doing may develop asthma or eczema from the strain. If encouraged, Six children will usually talk about their feelings, as long as they feel sure it's not going to upset anyone. As absent parents, Sixes are more reliable than most, turning up as promised and remembering birthdays.

CAREER

Having a good share of 'mother wit' these people need to find a position where it is respected. Most Sixes should be careful not to get stuck in a job where they have no status. It isn't just their snobbery that will be offended by this placement. The fact is that Sixes like to feel they are able to act as benefactors, and if they are only in a position to be recipients something inside them withers. Any post where diplomacy is needed may suit – sometimes literally as a diplomat (especially in the case of Librans) or as personnel officers. Anything involving healing, in however roundabout fashion, is likely to appeal. They make good doctors, vets and market gardeners. Whatever job they accept they need to feel sure there is room for them to 'do good' in some way, and this is not hard as they are quite inventive about finding ways to do this.

Sixes work hard, although they are not usually keen to work through their coffee break unless for a really good cause. It seems important to them to keep a sense of balance. However, if they are engaged on a challenging project they will want desperately to do their best and so may over-exert themselves. They like to be absorbed in their work. Also they like their work surroundings to be peaceful and aesthetically pleasing, or they do not feel able to concentrate. Excessive criticism will upset them, although a constructive remark may be well-received. Sixes are always looking to improve themselves and their efficiency. They like to feel respected by their colleagues and will find it hard to endure a situation where they are not.

In the workplace Sixes respect tradition and accept authority, providing it is fair. They think for themselves, but keep their thoughts to themselves unless extremely provoked. They like to help and encourage their subordinates, but can be extremely huffy if there is any hint of rebellion. They are not overly ambitious but take pleasure in a job well done. They are often best placed in middle management, where they can mediate between the commands from 'on high' and the people below them. Thus they are able to get the best from all concerned. They will often take pleasure in making tea

and buying cakes for their colleagues, as long as this is seen as caring, not demeaning.

Sixes who decide to work for themselves need to be sure that the job itself is fulfilling and answers their need to 'help'. It will be hard for them to feel motivated by money alone. Sixes are generally good with money, having a realistic sense of what they need and exactly how far the money will go, although they are sometimes tempted to overspend by things of great beauty.

Sixes are peaceful people and many a group in society has had cause, probably unbeknownst, to be grateful for their soothing effect. A Six who has learnt to work with some discord in order to create a harmony that is bone-deep, not skin-deep, really is a healer of the first water.

MAKING THE BEST OF YOURSELF

You may not be perfect, but you wouldn't be human if you were – honestly! It would be far better if you could stop wasting energy trying to match up to your own expectations.

The whole idea of 'making the best of yourself' is one you may, if you aren't careful, twist round and use to make the worst of yourself. By this I mean it may result in more attempts to appear faultless – and therefore less of the genuine you.

Where is it written that you have to cope smilingly with everything, never appear angry or envious, always have the *bon mot* and the helping hand? You are acceptable, warts and all. Of course, you won't believe this, so perhaps you need a little practice. So decide that once every day you'll say how you really feel. 'No, I'm sorry, I can't go to the shop for you today, because I'm too busy.' Or, 'You know it really makes me angry when you interrupt me like that.' No worthwhile relationship will ever be harmed by that sort of honesty, and that's something that you won't discover unless you try it.

If you are the sort of Six that seems to run round like a scalded duck (a graceful scalded duck, of course) doing everything for everyone but yourself and having little sense of 'the meaningful' then the best thing to do is take a holiday to disengage yourself from that sort of

behaviour. While you're away, use the time to sort out what you do and don't want to continue with, and work out a step-by-step approach to disengage. There are all sorts of polite and harmonious ways to go about this, and if you give yourself time to think of them you'll see how resourceful you are.

Society depends on people like you to cement it, and it is your nature to be helpful. Remember, being 'nice' may well not be meeting your real needs, and unless these are satisfied your ability to be of genuine help will be limited.

COMPATIBILITIES

On the surface, Sixes are so easy-going that they may seem to get on with anyone. Ones provide stimulation, and a harmonious partnership is possible with a Four. Threes can find a haven of peace with a Six and this often works well. They are sometimes somewhat bland for Sevens. Eights and Twos are best bets for a happy life.

VISUALISATION

Relax totally as described in the Introduction.

You have ventured out far into the grounds of a country house where you are staying. The house is a good five minutes' walk away. It is late afternoon, pleasantly warm. You feel very relaxed, wandering among the flowering shrubs, trees and hedges. The grass is smooth and green. Here and there you come across elegant statues. The scent of roses fills the air, as they are growing profusely beside all the paths.

Finding a lily-paved pond in front of a summer-house you stop in admiration. A fountain sprays gently over the blooms and leaves of the lilies. It issues from a chalice held by a statue of the Goddess. You linger to enjoy the serenity and the solitude.

Suddenly the sky darkens and big thunder-drops splash on your head and shoulders. You move into the summer-house and watch

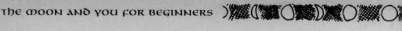

as the storm gathers. Blue-black clouds marshal overhead and lightning begins to play. As the thunder booms and the rain crashes down all over the garden, roaring on the roof of the summer-house. It seems to be wrecking the lovely garden. All the roses hang their bedraggled heads. The gentleness of the fountain is lost in the deluge.

But there is a beauty in the power of the storm. Perhaps you may like to step out under the warm drops, close your eyes and be part of it all. Let the wildness flow through you, banishing all the cobwebs, perhaps washing away some unwanted notions also. Allow yourself to be energised by the lightning flashes.

Whether you have ventured into the storm or have remained in the summer-house, affirm three times, 'I am perfectly balanced. My acceptance of strife strengthens my harmony.'

The storm clears as quickly as it came and the garden sparkles anew in the slanting sunbeams. You also feel sparkling and new. You can now come back to everyday consciousness, or return to the house, where your hostess waits, and see what else may be revealed to you there. Whatever you decide, bring the feeling of being cleansed and renewed back with you into ordinary life. Write down anything you would like to remember.

OTHER TYPE SIXES

Chopin, W. B. Yeats, George Harrison, Bryan Ferry, Jimi Hendrix, Shelley, William Blake.

EARTHLY HARMONIES

Colours   Deep rose, most soft shades of pink, soft blues, violet.
Oils, flowers, herbs   Calamus, gardenia, geranium, sweet pea, eucalyptus.
Stones   Rose quartz, selenite, celestite, pink, green or blue tourmaline, sodalite.

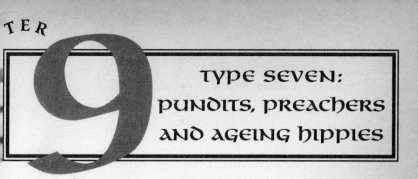

TYPE SEVEN:
PUNDITS, PREACHERS
AND AGEING HIPPIES

Then said a teacher: Speak to us of
Teaching. And he said: No man can
reveal to you ought but that which
already lies in the dawning of your
knowledge . . .

Kahlil Gibran, *The Prophet*

You'll find them on soap-boxes at Speakers' Corner, or gesticulating in smoky cafés amid a circle of serious faces. Often, without knowing it, you will read what they have written, or be taking notes at a lecture given by them. Wise, witty, tedious or irritating, these people have some sort of message to give, and they have just got to enlarge upon it. Of course not every Seven will be extroverted or confident enough to command an audience, but if they're not doing it outwardly you may be sure its going on inside – a weighing of ideas, an exploration of implications, a crystallisation of opinions.

If you want to seek out obscure meanings, from the Bardo Thodol to the symbology of a Mills and Boon plot, an intelligent Seven is your recommended guide. They tend to feel there's a moral in everything, if only one can find it. If they don't know much about the particular subject, then they are sure to know a person or book that can help. Failing this, your average Seven will be happy to accompany you on a treasure hunt for further knowledge. For a Seven the crock of gold is finding out more about what they actually believe, going deeper into it all, getting to the 'Aha!' or 'Eureka!' that comes when something is known throughout one's entire being.

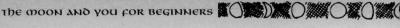

Of course not every Seven will be an Archimedes, but most of them feel they have a mission, even if it is only to sort out the neighbourhood cats. The dynamic behind this is a drive to 'sort out' their own ideas and beliefs. At this point in the Moon's phases she is a way-worn half-disc in the dark sky of the small hours. The cycle is drawing to a close, but the end is not yet in sight. The last stages are embarked upon, before final decline. At this point we ask ourselves, 'What has it all meant?' A philosophy needs to be formed, a belief validated in order to have the courage to face the darkness. Sevens are literally born in the light of this.

In our ideas of the Goddess, now is the waxing time of the waning. This is the first of the Crone stages. As wise woman, herbalist, midwife and matchmaker, she tends human affairs. It is the instinct of most Sevens to be involved and relevant. Ever and anon, to feel at peace inside they come back to the stirring, the mixing, and the weighing, the sweeping and the sorting. They tend to feel at their most relaxed when nearly 'there'. When the argument has been formulated, the end achieved, they get the niggling feeling that they must go further and beyond, to find other matters to set to rights.

Sevens can be great reformers and will often speak up for the underdog, even at their own peril. Seeing a small girl being taunted by two larger companions, one elderly Seven lady raised her folded umbrella (more as a gesture than a weapon) and waded in to her defence. Luckily this lady was as agile physically as she was mentally. She was only just in time to dodge the flying feet of one of the big girls, as Titch began to swing her round by the hair! Sevens need to think before embarking on a crusade.

Sevens can become quite fanatical. If they feel they have found the answer they can become a pain trying to convert all and sundry to their beliefs. Their zeal can make them deaf to other points of view, making them bigoted. Of course, bigotry is what they truly despise because it bars the way to knowledge. While some Sevens earnestly avoid any suspicion of dogmatism, for this reason, others are simply unable to perceive their own stubbornness because it is too dreadful to acknowledge. These people can be really indestructible! Usually the worst they do is bore people, but extreme fanaticism can be scary if not balanced by common sense.

Most Sevens, however, are humanitarian and have active social consciences. It is typical of them to campaign for recycling centres and speed bumps, and to walk tirelessly from house to house collecting for Amnesty International. They have a profound conviction that there is a way to make the world a better place, although sometimes they get very fed up and negative about it all, through frustration. Many Sevens have an evangelical side, and while this may literally be expressed as the espousal of a particular creed, it can just as easily manifest as a love of beautiful things – music, sculpture, or just the charm of wood, hill and lake. Inside them they feel that if only they could impart the sheer wonder of it all to others, that would be the answer to so much, from wife-battering to world war. At their best, Sevens really do have something in their soul that inspires, and if they are able to convey this they can certainly start things happening.

Sevens have a great fear of being misunderstood, and that is often their fate in early life. Motivated by all sorts of things they can't quite understand and could never convey, tense because of their inner struggles, they can appear awkward and antisocial. Sometimes they act superior and end up alone, which they hate. Often they fall foul of peers and authority. They can never quite manage to dress fashionably. They say things that get up the noses of their elders. Badly, sadly they need to be acknowledged. Stranded between two worlds they may fear they are going to be misfits all their life, and that feels like a real tragedy because deep down they know they have something really valuable to contribute. Meet them as they approach mid-life, however, and you are likely to see someone who is really clued up about things that matter to them and who has achieved some status within their circle. Strongly individualistic, they may convey this by choice of clothes or in their mannerisms. Often they know how to make an impression. It is the strength of Sevens to learn from their struggles and mistakes, and then to help others learn through them. They are great broadcasters of knowledge.

Sevens are not the easiest of people to get close to, although it may seem at first as if they are opening themselves like a book to your gaze. The truth of the matter is you'll only be seeing what they want you to see. As they quite quickly learn the value of self-knowledge,

they are in a position to decide which parts of themselves they are prepared to expose. They may well experience the world as potentially critical and after some hard knocks in early life they know how to protect themselves. No one (except perhaps a Nine) realises more clearly than a Seven that knowledge is power. Self-knowledge is the greatest power of all, and it is something that most Sevens achieve, to a greater or lesser extent. It is certainly somthing they work at, perhaps even more than knowing about others.

Sevens can become quite agitated at times. In fact the word has to be used – they can be neurotic. They are apt to blow things up out of all proportion, because sorting out the world and themselves can become such a demanding task. Often they feel an inner compulsion to achieve, achieve, achieve. This can take place in the privacy of their own homes, or souls. It certainly does not have to mean an upwardly mobile direction in a company hierarchy.

However, Sevens need to feel they are getting somewhere in terms of their own deeper values. They have to feel they amount to something or they have a horrid, sinking feeling, as if there is a leak in them somewhere that they must find and plug, before too much is lost. In a word they can be anxious. Perhaps all of the Phases this one needs a vocation, a true calling where they can actualise their ideals, for although they dream endlessly they are rarely content if they do only that.

Sevens at their best can have extensive influence, for they can be charismatic. If they have found something worth saying, people will listen and they can be extremely dynamic when fired by some vision. At their worst they can be tired nags, forever raising weary eyes to the skies, deploring the folly of their companions.

It is up to each Seven to realise the power they have – for when they come into their own they are powerful people, and not to blame society and other people for their lack of achievement. Sevens who have learnt not to waste energy by thrashing around or to expect to accomplish too much too soon (very much a Seven trait) can bring about some fundamental changes in society in general or in their chosen sphere.

RELATIONSHIPS

The tendency Sevens have to take things seriously very definitely extends to their love life. They often go overboard for someone who seems to embody an ideal, and like Eights they can turn their lover into a god. Their capacity for sacrifice and devotion is remarkable. They may see a type of 'saviour' in their lover – someone who can open doors to enchanted realms and light up their life. To a Seven in love the world is transformed. Mythological figures seem to walk the earth. Lancelot and Guinevere, Menelaus with his Helen – they surely never soared to the dizzy peaks of a Seven, on the wings of passion! In these circumstances Sevens often feel that their partnership really can change the world. Together they will make magic, do great things.

This is all larger than life, and exciting though it is it can play havoc with the lives of Sevens and those they are involved with. Being loved by a Seven may be a bit scary and the weight of all their projected fantasies may be too heavy to bear. Some Sevens frighten off potential partners by appearing to expect too much. Superficial affairs will not often hold much joy for them, unless Gemini is strong, or perhaps Aries and Sagittarius. They often suffer because partners cannot or will not help them build their dreams and enter them with them. The average Seven is not tailor-made for 'a bit on the side' and few types are more shattered by deceit.

Throwing themselves so completely into relationships can put Sevens in positions that are hard to retrieve. If things go wrong they can be left stranded on the tide of their enthusiasm. One Seven woman, disillusioned by her current relationship, found a man in strong contrast to the outgoing partner. Typically she was given to extremes – A was All Wrong, so B must be All Right. In a few months she had sold up and moved herself and her children eighty miles away, to be with Mr Wonderful. When it dawned on her that none of his promises were going to materialise she alternated between panic and despair.

Practicality is not often Seven's strongest suit, and at this point Sevens are prone to get religion, or take to alcohol as a way out. A

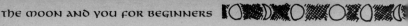

more effectual approach is for Sevens to dream possible dreams, thereby creating an atmosphere conducive to positive change – a course this woman did adopt, after much angst. She was lucky. Soon she was able to make an equally dramatic but much wiser move back home. Determined to learn from her mistakes, she is now able to give guidance to others on the basis of her experience. Naturally she is in her element.

Being loved by a Seven can feel like a responsibility. Unlike Eights, Sevens do expect things. These are rarely purely material, but Sevens want to see their dreams made flesh, at least in part. It is possible for a partner to fall off the perch a Seven has provided. To see the spark snuffed out in the eyes of a Seven is a horrible thing. However, keeping the magic alive is not as hard as some may think. All you need to do is to step into their dreamworld with them, and to understand that what they really need from you is that you act as a catalyst for whatever alchemy currently engages them. For behind all the larger-than-life stuff is the power of Sevens' imagination, which they can use to enrich the relationship and daily life unilaterally, rather than expecting a reincarnation of Valentino or Cleopatra.

Sex is something that Sevens, on the whole, take seriously. At some level they see it as sacred. It is as if the entire cosmos is condensed into the loving union. Tantra and sex magic may attract them, and they 'get off on' declarations of unending passion, such as 'You and I were written in the stars.' Usually they prefer one partner – after all, how can this be the love to end all loves if one of you is messing around with someone else? However, in their drive to get past the threshold of ordinary experience, some Sevens do experiment with more than one lover, in the belief that we are all manifestations of the divine. Maybe if they do this or that they will achieve the ultimate high. There is a streak of 'try anything' in some Sevens, and this could extend to some questionable sexual activities. These are likely to pall when realisation dawns that they are a pathway to distaste rather than transcendence.

Life with a Seven is unlikely to be predictable but at its best it can turn into a ceaseless celebration, a festival of wine and moonlight, a sacrament of the sensual. Of course it will have its mundane side,

but you can cope with burnt toast and rising mortgages if you fix your eyes on a star.

FAMILY LIFE

Many Sevens see their families as a ready-made theatre to play out all their new ideas for setting things straight. Here there is a captive audience, people close to them that they can really influence, so it can be done as it should be done!

As parents, Sevens can be embarrassing. They don't dress their age, and often they don't look it. In their wish to be acceptable, to get across to younger people and to be noticed, they may adopt fashions that owe nothing to Marks & Spencer! While their own son or daughter disowns them by walking ten paces ahead in the High Street, other children and teenagers find them fascinating, and will often seek them out for advice on things they couldn't possibly tell their own parents.

The ideas of Sevens are often avant-garde. Teenage sex and drugs don't phase them – indeed they may try out the latter (or even the former) themselves. However, they do like to be listened to. It distresses them if their children do not respect their ideals and beliefs. Often their children can't quite take advantage of what is on offer, for children without realising it look for some rigidity in order to feel secure. The excess of liberalism can be unsettling. A Seven parent must not be pushed too far, however, or a bedrock of dogmatism may be reached. Sevens care very deeply. Their broad-mindedness is not a *laissez-faire* but the result of extensive thought.

Loving to teach their children, Sevens can get carried away in this. One Seven Mum was asked by her little girl where she had 'come from'. Strongly believing that sex should be an open subject, Seven Mum was well prepared. She launched into the saga of sperms and eggs, interspersed with comments about the importance of love and respect. The little girl listened patiently, and at the end of it all said in a small voice, 'That was very interesting, Mummy, but Becky comes from Birmingham, so I wondered where I come from.' Sevens' feet have a habit of straying into their mouths!

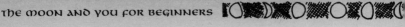

More than any other, Type Seven children must be listened to. Often they are extremely wise and quick to spot inconsistencies, or to read between the lines. Adults are often an open book to them, and that is not an endearing trait. Contemporaries may find them boring and teachers aggravating. They need the respect and support of their parents if they are to find a way of fitting in with everyone else.

Sevens will often welcome step-families as long as they are given status and their own place. A Seven step-mum can cope brilliantly with the love problems of a teenage daughter, but if she feels she is usurped in any way there will be fireworks. Seven stepchildren may seem unreachable. They should not be patronised. Give them some true attention and they will blossom. As absent parents, Sevens are not perfect. Their sense of their own importance may be threatened by the new family, and they may prefer to forge ahead with a new life, leaving the old behind them as far as they are able (which will never be totally). They can also be pretty good at thinking up excellent morally sound reasons why they should not be liable for maintenance! However, it is characteristic of them to produce generous gifts.

Families are great things to philosophise about and Sevens will go to town on this. Having a strong sense of family, they are often active members. Sometimes they are out of touch with the way things really are, as they are too busy seeing something ideal. None the less they usually work hard in this area.

CAREER

Perhaps more than any other phase, Sevens need to feel that their job is basically worthwhile. Not all can have a vocation in the accepted sense, although there is much in their temperament that lends itself to social work, teaching and writing. However, it is rarely enough for a Seven to fulfil the urge to disseminate ideas completely outside their work itself. This means that the supermarket checkout operator will not be content to tell her colleagues about what she has been reading or gossip with customers, although she may enjoy doing both. She will need to feel that helping people to buy food is worthwhile in itself, and she may well extend this to promoting the

recipe leaflets often supplied by food shops. Sevens hate and despise work they consider petty, and in those circumstances there is no more disgruntled employee.

Many Sevens are driven to be creative in some form. In this they are rarely content, feeling they have to push themselves to ever greater output, as if they need to justify their own existence. They need to prove themselves to society and they yearn for approval and a sense of achievement. Sevens can become very depressed if they feel their talents are unexpressed, and in this they often create their own barriers and see opposition where none exists. Inside they probably lack confidence, although this is rarely obvious. Secretly they may prefer seclusion but they know that if they crawl into a hole they may never come out – and that feels dire indeed.

Although conscious of the value of money, Sevens can be extravagant. Periods of intense saving may alternate with spending sprees, so their finances may not achieve an even keel. Often they are 'penny wise and pound foolish'. They see the need for boundaries although they may find them hard to keep within.

It is the task of Sevens to explore meanings and to interpret them for the rest of us. Whether this is done largely and significantly or on a modest, barely noticeable scale will depend on their abilities. Sometimes obscure, far-fetched and fanatical, often very funny, they are rarely predictable. If they cultivate 'reverence with mirth' they can be fascinating companions.

MAKING THE BEST OF YOURSELF

Chances are that any typical Seven will turn to this page avidly, all antennae trembling for info! How can I improve myself? What have I missed that I should know? Could this be the key to unlock the final door, so now I will have all the answers?

Definitely not. So just stop for a moment, and ask yourself what you're trying to prove. Is there a critical voice inside you that whispers you're an idiot – and is that why you try to have all the answers? If so where does that voice come from? Try to recognise your own self-destructive side, the part of you that may prevent you

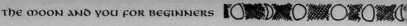

from enjoying your achievements, that may be blocking your path to wisdom by the uncertainty it engenders.

The way to true self-improvement is to spend some time discovering what it is you really want to achieve for yourself, and that is no simple matter, for most of us have many layers of expectation and conditioning muffling the still small voice that trills, 'This is me!' It is very easy to say this, and it has been so often repeated that it has become a cliché – but it is still true. Of course, it is true for us all, not just for Sevens. However, a typical Seven – with their nose for dissection and dissemination – is wonderfully suited to positive self-analysis, and is better employed that way than on some less useful quest. So take the time and look inwards. There is as much beauty and meaning there as you will ever find outside, and you will be so much better equipped to appreciate the external if you are acquainted with the internal.

If you are a Seven who seems to get eternally bogged down with thankless charity work and the trivia of minor committees, you need to realise that your vital resources are dribbling away, draining you, but never making any waves – and the only way to stop this is to disengage. It may feel painful, because Sevens' involvements can feel as precious as a limb. Amputation is the only answer, and once you get involved in writing that book, studying that new subject or running for the local council, believe me, you won't feel a twinge. You can't do everything, but you can make a real difference to something if you restrict and focus your efforts.

Most Sevens have a strong instinct to understand, make a stand and impart what they know. They will do all of this best if they bear in mind the major instruction of the Eleusinian mysteries: 'Know Thyself'.

COMPATIBILITIES

Sevens are great with Eights, who can share their ideals (and embody them sometimes) without undue strain and competition. Sixes and Fours may make them impatient, and there could be clashes with Nines and Threes. With Ones and Twos the partnership could be dynamic and Fives often fascinate them.

VISUALISATION

Relax yourself, as described in the Introduction.

You are following a forest path – picture yourself walking, or riding a horse. The sky is gradually lightening from the East and through the overhead branches the half-disc of the waning Moon glows palely golden. Smell the earthy scents that rise from the forest floor. Feel the freshness of the morning stealing in on a gentle breeze. Breathe deeply – breathe this fresh, invigorating scent, allow it to pulsate in your veins. Feel yourself becoming more energetic, more alive.

You begin to hear the sound of water tinkling and you come upon a crystal stream. In the pale light the ripples twinkle in silver and gold. Stop or dismount. Trail your hands in the water, bathe your face or drink of it. It has a milky coolness and also an electric charge that sends shivers of delight through you. You go on your way feeling refreshed in spirit.

Now you come out of the wood and find yourself at the top of an escarpment. The sky is becoming paler, but stars are still shining. The Moon is watching overhead. For miles and miles around the shadowed landscape stretches around you. You can see the purple horizon, and in a dip between the hills the sea reflects a golden pathway cast by the Moon. Rising and falling on the swell rides a sailing ship. The ship waits for you. At your right hand is what you take to be a large rock. Slowly you become aware that it is the figure of an old woman, wrapped in a cloak. An aura of deep peace surrounds her. Absorb this peace, feel accepted. You may like to speak to her. If she answers, take special note of what she says.

As you stand before this sweeping panorama, allow yourself to feel the huge range of possibilities life contains. Take the breadth of it deeply into you and let it become part of you. Be aware of the enormous potential you have, and let yourself feel you can do anything you reasonably dream of. Affirm three times, 'I have nothing to prove. In joy I fulfil my dreams.'

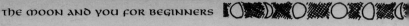

Feeling enriched and enlivened you may now slowly come back to everyday awareness. Or if you wish you may travel down to the ship and see where it takes you. The old woman may accompany you. Remember, this is no ordinary ship. It is designed to ferry you to new realisations rather than distant lands. Wherever you go, allow yourself in due time to bring back to everyday life what you have gathered, and to feel energetic and renewed.

OTHER TYPE SEVENS

Buddy Holly, Nijinsky, Edith Piaf, Carl Jung, Nikolai Lenin.

EARTHLY HARMONIES

Colours   Wine, crimson, fuchsia, blue-green, turquoise and navy, sometimes gold and silver.
Oils, flowers, herbs   Grape, lotus, clove, honeysuckle, maple, lavender.
Stones   Sapphire, rutilated quartz, amazonite, sugilite, sardonyx, jade.

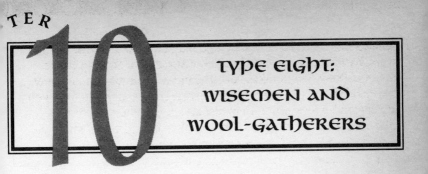

TYPE EIGHT: WISEMEN AND WOOL-GATHERERS

The wind is old and still at play
While I must hurry upon my way
For I am running to Paradise.

W. B. Yeats, 'Running to Paradise'

The person whose eyes rarely focus on what they're looking at, who tells of his dreams and spills the cornflakes at breakfast, and who often seems to be in confusion yet seldom comes a cropper – this is the picture of Type Eight. Frequently they give the impression of trying hard to 'connect' but never quite making it – and not really minding. Their inner world is often so fascinating to them that they'd rather not leave it. However, they'll smile so benignly at you when you speak to them that the chances are you'll never consider they're not hearing a word you say.

The meaning of life and the purpose of existence are things that preoccupy these people. They are as capable as the next person of being practical – well almost. This is the surgeon who sews you up with a swab still inside, or the mechanic who leaves a spanner under your bonnet. Yet the same surgeon has wonderful healing abilities and a superb bedside manner. After all, the swab didn't really affect the success of the operation. As for your car, it's never gone better. It's just that you wondered what that funny rattling was.

Type Eights are people that you never really get to know. It's not that they're purposely concealing anything. Their beatific ear-to-ear grin usually confirms that. There are simply things they can't convey and couldn't if they tried. There's a mystery about them. However, they do tend to have an uncanny way of knowing exactly what's going on in your mind. This could upset some people except that Eights are so charming and caring about it that you just know they've only exposed your sore point so they could pour balm in precisely the right place.

Some Eights do literally opt for a life of seclusion, for the Moon is now approaching her darkness. Now is the time of the Hidden, a time for quiet and rest. This is the 'full' time of the waning stage. Peace is sought and the fruits of the imagination and the inner world are there to be gathered. The Goddess, as Crone, retreats to embroider her tapestry of the elusive images of the heart, or stirs her cauldron, humming softly. The instincts of typical Eights are to cultivate a vivid inner life, and this is where they find their home. Reality to them is sometimes nebulous. They know that things are not what they seem and exhortations like 'Wake up!' or 'Concentrate!' can strike them as meaningless. They may feel deeply violated by anything that seeks to disrupt or invade this inner landscape, for it is there that they are building the castle of their security, in their own way. It often has little to do with bricks and mortar.

Eights are acutely aware of the infinite – as are Sevens and Nines, which is what we all must face in the end. Entering the priesthood or a nunnery, or becoming an initiate into ways of more pagan wisdom can give Eights a reassuring framework for the eternal realities they sense. If something of this sort is not found Eights can find that their inexpressible inner experience becomes a lonely burden in a world that prefers to deny it.

Whatever way they follow, Eights are rarely judgmental or condemnatory. One elderly Catholic priest, having been a faithful scion of the Church all his life, was heard to murmur that he was sure the Pope would one day realise there was no Hell, and say so. It was the spirit behind his faith, not the dogma that he had tended for so many years.

Of course few Eights will actually enter a contemplative order, but most are touched by eternity whatever walk of life they tread. They will regularly stop to watch a glorious sunset, or take a poignant

tune into their very bones. Whether they are talented or not they will have an artistic streak that will extend to appreciation, if nothing else. Often they write poetry. Although they may be happy with their own company they are often sought by others.

This particular phase lends itself to drama. The fact that 'all the world's a stage' is something they perceive as a daily reality and so an actual theatre can seem as relevant to them as daily life. Symbology and cryptic meanings are inherent in theatre, as is a sense of the ephemeral (the play will come to an end). A play is specifically and consciously what routine existence may be unconsciously – full of hidden meanings. At least that is how Eights perceive it. A play is also fun, and that's how many Eights prefer to see life. Lots of Eights take to stage performance like ducks to water. At the very least they will love to watch.

There is a saying that no one ever uttered on their death-bed that they wish they'd spent more time at the office. Eights have more chance of achieving death-bed peace than most of us, because they are more generally aware of real values. Of course Eights as much as anyone else are affected by the demands of modern life and they can certainly be found pondering company statistics by the light of the midnight oil. They are not made for this, however, and may become quite overwrought if pushed to behave in this way. Mostly they have an irrepressible sense of fun. 'Eat, drink and be merry, for tomorrow we die,' sounds inside them – but the emphasis is on the 'merry'. Eights have a ready laugh (even if you're not always sure what was funny, and wonder if it was you) and will happily take time out to play.

If all the foregoing makes Eights sounds like a cross between Buddha and Rolf Harris perhaps we should also note how stubborn they can be. Whereas the waxing Moon types are more prone to go their own way unstoppably, waning types tend more to dig in their heels and defend their own bit of ground. Eights have a gentle awareness that 'all things must pass' and the stuff that sends most of us tearing about is just so much white noise to them. Benign and bewildered, they watch from the wings, sometimes sad and guilty that they can't join in. However, push them too hard to conform and

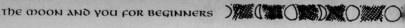

they will simply stonewall. They can't explain their point of view and they don't expect it to be respected in a materialistic world, but they know what they know and they won't be budged. Try to force them and they'll go deeper into their shell and you'll get nothing from them. You have to respect their views to coax out their wisdom.

Let's also not forget their sense of guilt. Quite a lot gets by your average Eight (although little of true import escapes them). Often they have a sneaking feeling that they're missing something they ought to take on board.

However, it's more that that. Remember, the Moon is in the last-but-one stage in her rotation. A vast amount of experience has been assimilated in the cycle and sometimes Eights may carry an awareness of the entire range of human mistakes and ills. It's as if they have the whole world on their shoulders. They may translate this literally into a feeling that it's 'all their fault' and decide it is their task single-handedly to put everything right, from their sister's failing marriage to the hole in the ozone layer. There may be a little egotism involved in this. With as much inward know-how as Eights possess it's hard not to feel you know best. However, like the rest of us, Eights can get it wrong. Sometimes they need to learn not to meddle.

Another favourite Eight occupation is worry. Of course so much can go awry, and Eights know it. Not for them the forward thrust and trust of the waxing phases. The man who drives at a steady 30 mph (but less when not on a motorway) in a reinforced car, wearing a crash helmet, is probably an Eight, turned neurotic by endless rumination. However, it is just when Eights go to such extremes that they do court disaster. What a New Moon possesses in faith in life Eights can make up for by faith in the eternal. Then they have their very own Guardian Angel.

Eights can be lucky. There's something about the playful detachment with which they approach life when at their best that attracts good fortune. It is said that 'you make your own luck' and if by nothing else Eights do this through their indefinable charm.

RELATIONSHIPS

Type Eights are usually quite easy-going in relationships. When things go wrong their reaction is often to distance themselves. Deep down they are aware that human emotions are endlessly complex and so it seems that the simplest thing to do is to hope the trouble will go away. However, this 'rolling over and playing dead' can be enraging to a partner who desperately needs their emotions to be recognised. Type Eight relationships sometimes wither and die while they take up the 'ostrich position'.

It isn't that Eights don't care – far from it. Their feelings run very deep, connected as they are to a mystical source within them. They prefer a peaceful life and are disturbed by the thought of what may be thrown up by a conflict. Also they do not like to get hurt or to cause hurt. Somewhere inside them there is a feeling that 'it doesn't matter anyway'. Yes, the partnership matters (to a greater or lesser extent) but in the end humans and their passions, all that we build from home to empire are as permanent as the leaves on the trees. Eights know that it is love that counts, in an abstract sense. It does not really matter whether someone cast a glance at the stunning blond – of either sex – or forgot someone's birthday. (Eights are quite liable to do the latter.) This attitude is not understood by many people and Eights need to come down from the clouds and really think about how they are behaving to loved ones, rather than worrying absently because they feel something is wrong.

Eights have a wonderful way of putting their lovers on pedestals and keeping them there. This is no uncomfortable perch, but a glorious wallow in the Type Eight dream-scene. They genuinely do not notice minor faults. They need their fantasy, their bit of heaven-on-earth. Give them something to build on and they'll embellish it to their requirements and you will be treated like a god or goddess. They can be very romantic – even if the bouquet of red roses doesn't actually coincide with the anniversary. Eights may need a bit of a push to start the romance, however. You may have been in their dreams for months without ever getting a whisper of it, but give them the 'green light' and they'll go into action so smoothly that it's obvious the hesitation didn't stem from embarrassment alone.

Eights will generally be faithful unless bitterly disillusioned or betrayed. If that does happen they will see scant reason why they should not deceive, if they so wish and the opportunity arises. Their rose-coloured specs are pretty indestructible, but if they are shattered Eights may go where they can't be retrieved and that could well be into someone else's arms.

When it comes to erotic fantasy, Eights come into their own, and if they really 'loosen up' they are willing to tell stories and play roles when love-making. A little harmless bondage and enacting master/slave may appeal, but don't be surprised if it turns into a bit of a giggle! Also Eights can be very imaginative when it comes to grapes and ice-cream and interesting ways to use them! Eights make wonderful, gentle lovers, and are good at tuning in to what a partner wants. They will try almost anything, but sometimes it may seem that their passion lacks an 'edge'. Never think it's because they're low on libido or don't fancy you. It's just that their 'if it doesn't happen today it'll happen tomorrow' attitude can pervade even their love-making. If you care about them you will soon find the right way to turn them on.

Eights indulge more in auto-erotic behaviour than most. It enables them to lose themselves in a fantasy world, and this is not always to be recommended, for it is no substitute for the loving relationship that Eights truly crave. They need to give themselves a push to go out and join the real world, for it's only by contact with others that their dreams really acquire wings.

On occasion Eights find themselves victims in relationships. Because they are undemanding and accommodating, not liking to 'rock the boat' they can be subject to abuse. In this they suffer horribly, not only in the obvious way, but also because their tender dreams are shredded and their sense of the aesthetic trampled upon. However, they have various means of escape. One woman, abused by her bullying boyfriend found that she could escape her misery in a unique way. By concentrating upon some inanimate object such as the wardrobe, she felt able to project her 'essence' into it, partake of its solidity and feel thereby assured that she would eventually escape – which she did.

Eights have mysterious ways of operating. Don't think you can understand them because that's doubtful, especially if you were born within a waxing phase. Nor can you ever quite possess an Eight. Maybe it's this quality that frustrates and provokes abuse. But if they are badly treated they will slip away. Their elusiveness is fascinating, but trusting in them brings rich rewards.

FAMILY LIFE

Don't expect your Type Eight child to remember lunch or homework. Of course he will most of the time, which further complicates matters. He or she rarely gets into trouble, however, and if the lunch is still on the doormat someone is sure to share theirs with him, just so they can bask in that smile for a moment. Another thing that may be forgotten accidentally-on-purpose is the PE kit. Eights are generally not attracted to sport unless they can excel at it and all goes smoothly. Then it will take its place as a great means of escape.

Speaking of escape – which we frequently do with Eights – fantasy is of prime importance to this child. They can lose themselves in film plots which they then recount in detail, despite the fact they may have difficulty remembering their address! These children need to be read to perhaps more than any other type, and they must be listened to when they speak of their inner world. Ensure their shelves are filled with all manner of books, from Roald Dahl to C. S. Lewis, and when they tell you about the ghost they saw, or the monster in the moonlight, get them to write it down. They need some way of grounding themselves, and while this will be reasonably easy for a Taurus, Capricorn or Virgo Type Eight, others may disappear in the stratosphere without some focus.

Never trivialise or poo-pooh what they say – try to explore it with them so they can make their own sense out of it. Although they may be of a theoretical bent, Eights are often good at making models and taking things apart because they want to see deeply into how practical things work as well as abstracts. That needs to be encouraged.

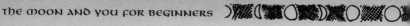

One little Type Eight girl caused her mother considerable worry because she persisted in talking about life, death and God on the way to school, every day, from the age of 5 onwards. Finding herself stretched by concepts like infinity and the survival of the ego in reincarnation ('If I come back in another body, Mummy, will I still feel like me?'), the mother banned all such discussions. Her daughter became withdrawn and her schoolwork deteriorated. One day her teacher called the mother to one side and told her that her child had been in tears in class. The reason for this turned out to be that the girl was worried about her mother's safety at home alone during the day.

In such a way Eights can become neurotic. If their need to explore hidden meanings is frustrated it will turn to worry. Also the little girl felt angry at her mother, then felt bad for feeling angry and so translated this to fear for mother's well-being. Eights do need to talk and explore or they will burrow like moles into their own Underworld. Fortunately this child's mother was wise enough not to inhibit further discussions and began to realise how stimulating the questions could be to her own ideas. Eights have this uncomfortable way of getting other people to look closely at themselves.

As children, Eights are mostly accommodating, only disobedient through absent-mindedness, and concerned for the harmony of the home. They sense this on an emotional level and may blame themselves when things go wrong, such as their parents' divorce. As siblings they can be irritating. One sore-pressed sister habitually addressed her Type Eight brother with the words 'Earth calling Sammy – come in please.' Sometimes he did, sometimes he didn't. Eights can use withdrawal as power.

Type Eight parents are accepting. Often they don't see mess, although they do get their children into helpful rhythms – it can hardly be called routine – they do sometimes fall short on the basics. If a child remembers his cookery class at the last minute and expects Type Eight Mum to have flour and sugar to hand – forget it! As for Dad, he'll still have his head under the car bonnet when his son should be half-way to football practice. When it comes to a bedtime story they are great, however, and will sometimes make up their own. Teenage problems, from broken hearts to drugs, are coped

with in a way that may seem laid back. However, Eights worry dreadfully over these things. It's just that they know there is no point laying down the law or saying, 'Pull yourself together.' In fact they are expert at steering their son or daughter out of danger and engendering the respect necessary for the process.

Adolescence poses comparatively few problems for Type Eight parents. After all, it's just another phase that comes and goes. They well remember their own adolescent agonies and can switch from feeling 36 to 6, 16 or 60 by a short step of the imagination. They have a way of soothing hurts, and if it often feels like they aren't there, when it really counts they are.

CAREER

Eights dream of what they will do when they grow up from a very early age, and this doesn't stop when they reach adulthood. They are future-oriented and fascinated by such things as what may be happening on other planets, and other planes. They have a sort of 'back to the future' mentality where past, present, future and the meaning of it all gets wound up in a fascinating tangle. Their ideas definitely aren't all whimsy. They have a way of seeing what others may have missed and often they have sound ideas for how things may be improved. Often they are ahead of their time at the same time as being caught in a sort of time-warp, which can make them seem quaint. They have a lot to contribute, even to most ordinary jobs.

Many Eights nurture a secret ambition to 'save the world'. In common with Sevens and Nines they are admirably suited to the role of counsellor or priest/ess. This need not be taken literally. Moon phase does not necessarily specify career choice or talent, but it will indicate needs and responses. Thus an Eight can turn her role of barmaid into a cross between psychiatrist and Mother-confessor. An Eight employed as a security guard could be playing St George, fighting the fight for the good and right as he strolls around Sainsbury's. Eights have a way of deepening and mythologising their experience.

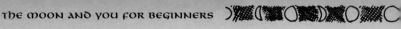

To be happy in their work, Eights need to see it as meaningful, either for itself, as perhaps a career as a counsellor might be, or for what they can make of it. A Type Eight prostitute will see herself as helping to prevent rapes and divorces, perhaps with some justification. Eights who work in offices will find their niche if they can interpret life for their colleagues. This is not a mother-hen instinct that wants to sort out everyone's problems. It's more a wish to 'justify the ways of God to Man' – and to themselves, of course.

Eights do not generally see their job solely in terms of financial reward. Unless they are heavily Capricornian or Taurean, hyacinths for the soul occupy them more than paying the bills. If forced to do a job they hate they will escape through day-dreaming. Often they cope with boring jobs better than most simply because they are able to find this outlet. However, if Eights are to make a great success of anything it needs to appeal to their imagination and they need to feel it matters.

Generally Eights are a bit vague about money. Five-pound notes turn up unexpectedly in pockets. Final demands for payment arrive before the original has been opened. However, they don't often get in a mess. It's as if they have an unconscious account book that keeps them solvent. Also they usually have an innate belief in luck. Some Eights seem gifted at winning money, to everyone's surprise but their own.

Eights are often content to interpret life quietly to those who will listen, and their full talent for this is not often expressed in youth. They, like anyone else, like to conform and if they find their 'esoteric' ways are not appreciated they will try to suppress them. An Eight who can find ways to express what he senses, either in words or actions is a valuable companion indeed. It is the role of Eights to lead by example, so that we can see other sides to the mundane and deepen our experience of life.

MAKING THE BEST OF YOURSELF

Now I know you know what I'm going to say, but I'm going to say it anyway. It's of little use having all these wonderful ideas if you don't

do something with them. And I know you're not completely content with feeling how rich life is with possibilities, how deeply meaningful it all is, and dreaming. Your dreams are what empower you, and give you your zest and ability to sort of celebrate it all – but you'll do this much better if you make something concrete of it, and deep down you know it.

So, what are your talents? Can you paint, draw, write, sculpt? Are you good at cooking, sewing, gardening? Do people come to you with their problems, to understand them or to make them laugh? Do you have a quick grasp of computers or cars? Whatever it is and however exotic or commonplace it may be, the chances are that this could be the starting point to 'build a dream'. Of course, the trouble with trying to actualise a dream is that you can't – and that's the hard part about it. In the process of making it real something has to be sacrificed – often quite a lot – and reality turns out to be a clumsy travesty of what you had envisaged. But this is something you have to live with. Your inner world will feel a better place to be if you can see some reflection of it, however dim, in the external. You can't save all the whales, but you can deliver leaflets for environmental pressure groups. You can't be van Gogh, but you can set aside a few hours a week to daub on a canvas.

Don't attempt to adopt a rigid routine, if you don't wish to, but be determined to have some time to do what is needed. Perhaps have a list of things to do and make sure you tackle it – in whatever order appeals. Be prepared to be active at any time you wish – you may feel things flow more for you after midnight, for instance. Also don't expect to achieve too much. Do just a little, regularly. Oak trees grow from acorns..

If you are an especially 'spaced out' Eight, who finds it almost impossible to relate to the ordinary or to be reasonably effectual, you need to ask yourself what you are avoiding, because absent-mindedness can be an excuse for not engaging with a world that is really making you angry and frustrated. Take note of your dreams and ask yourself what they mean. Explore books on symbols, psychology and the spiritual. Seek the help of friends and

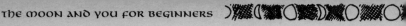

colleagues. Decide that you owe it to yourself to 'plug in' in some way. Eights are often fulfilled by inner solitary things, but that's not the same as idleness and drifting.

Although neither they nor others may be totally conscious of this, many Eights are an inspiration to those around them. But each Eight must firstly be an inspiration to her or himself.

COMPATIBILITIES

Eights do well to avoid Types One and Three as they are likely to annoy each other. Eights and Nines together are good, particularly for Nines, although at times the relationship could feel vague and/or murky. Eights get on well together and may share many dreams. For dynamism, Eights should pick a Seven, and for maximum harmony the choice would be a Six.

VISUALISATION

Relax yourself completely, as described in the Introduction.

Imagine that you are a tree. Your body forms the trunk, your head and hair are the branches, and your feet are the roots. Allow yourself time to feel the strength of the trunk that is your body. Feel the sensation of your feet spreading into the rich soil. Feel all the nourishment being taken up into you, strengthening your trunk, enabling your branches to reach higher and higher. Now imagine where your branches reach – where would they like to reach? There are no limits to the heights that you can attain, as this beautiful, magical tree. You can explore the upper reaches of the atmosphere, talk with jet-pilots or beings from other planets. You can reach the Moon. You can even send tendrils up to the sun and the stars. Allow your imagination free-rein and see what it reveals. All the while keep reminding yourself of your feet. They are rooted in earth. Allow what you experience to travel down your trunk to electrify your roots. Then feel them draw fresh goodness from the

soil. Feel this interplay between high-flying branch and deep-plunging root intensify as your tree grows from strength to strength. Affirm 'I can fly high and dream dreams, but I return to earth and plant them in the soil' three times. When you come out of the visualisation take with you the extra power you have gained, the belief in your dreams and their relationship to 'where you're at' – your roots.

OTHER TYPE EIGHTS

Leonardo da Vinci, Charles Dickens, Henri Toulouse-Lautrec, Richard Burton.

EARTHLY HARMONIES

Colours   Violet, purple, deep blues and greens.
Oils, flowers, herbs   Calamus, jasmine, lavender, violet, orris, anise, mimosa.
Stones   Mother-of-pearl, smoky quartz, amethyst, celestite, turquoise.

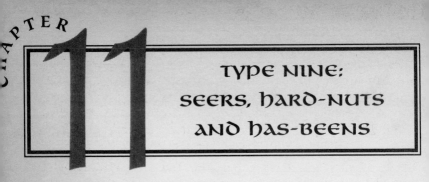

TYPE NINE: SEERS, HARD-NUTS AND HAS-BEENS

She is woman who sees ... She is crone woman
Deep earth cave mother, Dark moon blood mother ...
She is woman who knows ... Owl woman ... Old woman.

Carolyn Hillyer, 'Night Woman', from the album *House of the Weavers* and the book *Two Drumbeats: Songs of the Sacred Earth* (Seventh Wave Music, 1993)

If you're planning the rave-up of the year, best make sure that you don't invite too many Type Nines – that is unless you're organising a picnic in a midnight graveyard or a hop around the ouija board. In that case a Type Nine could be the soul, if not the life of the event, bringing a long face and plenty of cryptic comments instead of a bottle of wine!

Of course, this sounds grim, and indeed it's an extreme caricature. However, there can be a somewhat morose side to many Nines, although this may not be obvious. Like Eights they seem to be 'somewhere else' a lot of the time, and to have been just about everywhere else the rest of the time. It's as if they wear a tee-shirt saying 'Bin there, done that'. They are detached rather than dreamy. Hard to shock, they may at times seem impervious to much that may touch others deeply. Often difficult to communicate with, they walk a lonely path. Whatever place they occupy in the world there is a stony kernel to them, a dark heart whose secrets can only be hinted at.

At this stage of the Moon's rotation she is visibly at her weakest. She is lost in the dawn sky, while night is inky and forsaken. The cycle of experience that her movements represent is drawing to a close, and there remains only the question of ending. Of course, there is always the promise of rebirth, but as all wise Nines know, endings have to be fully experienced for rebirth to have meaning. This is a paradox – something with which Nines are at home.

The lunation cycle is drawing to a close. This is the waning time of the waning, a time of concealment, contraction and darkness. The message at this time is to let go, go beyond, go within. The Crone is at her most wizened and most secret. We can picture her deep within her cave, stirring, weaving, communing with spirits and guarding mysteries that all may seek but none can define. The instincts of Nines are often to find darkness in some form. This can be a very positive thing, where Nines face and grapple with what others may fear, and turn it – like latter-day alchemists – into their own special form of gold. Nines can accept human nature and face their own concealed parts, thus gaining great strength - or they can use their perceptions in a negative way, seeing decay and corruption and viewing all with suspicion. However, to feel 'at home' with themselves they need to be perpetually delving well below superficialities.

At their best, Nines carry a metaphorical beacon in the spirit that 'It is better to light a candle than to curse the darkness.' Their courage and willingness to face what most might shun are an inspiration. At their worst they trudge through life, shoulders hunched under the large chip they carry, letting everyone share their burdens by constantly complaining. Their life experience and the way they have handled it will determine which.

Nines tend to be old before their time. They possess an ever-present awareness of the foibles of their species and can be self-opinionated and suspicious. Taking nothing at face value they sometimes sniff and scrape until they have found the little piece of dry rot at the centre of the building. In the process they have probably done a good demolition job. Then they stand in bitter triumph amid the wreckage, saying, 'I told you it was rubbish.' Right again!

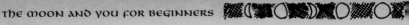

Whoever said 'Live well, that's the best revenge' was probably not a Nine. Few harbour a grudge in more fertile soil than a Nine who has been severely 'messed up'. As they will have concentrated much of their attention on others' weak spots they may well know just how to hurt. On the other hand, Nines at their best accept life's problems with fathomless serenity. The most vindictive people I have known were born at this phase, but also several of the bravest. Often they are prepared to face themselves, which is no easy matter for any of us. Their courage can be an inspiration to those with less guts and their loyalty, once bestowed, is second to none.

Type Nines can be magnetic or repellent. They may be both at different times, but they are rarely in between. One Type Nine, resigned to belonging to the latter group said, 'No one ever asks me to the pub for a drink. I'm not the sort.' This was said without self-pity, although he was undoubtedly lonely. It did not occur to him to modify the reserve that distanced others. Other Nines find themselves the centre of a respectful group and have friends for life. Nines are not good at changing, unless it is some fundamental change that they have decided themselves to initiate. They can be silently stubborn.

Nines are not keen on asking for help. Their motto is 'Every herring must hang by its own tail.' They know that in the end we are all alone, and that no one accompanies us out of this world. All we may take with us is our store of amassed wisdom. Nines can be extremely wise and willing to impart what they know to those they trust and who are able to understand. They like to help people find their own way. If you need someone to accompany you into the jaws of death, a good Nine is certainly your man or woman.

It is said, 'Judge not, lest ye yourself be judged.' It is typical of some Nines to utter such phrases with a portentous expression, at the same time as they are relentlessly judging! Nines perpetually feel that their souls are being weighed against a feather, and often they strive to do their best at the same time keeping their eyes on the meaning and purpose of it all. Some prefer to set themselves up as judges of others and as companions they have all the warmth of a moorland dolman! But such stones are reputed to have strange powers. Nines who have found themselves are powerful people.

Nines are often attracted to the mysterious, or the 'basic'. Some may have a specific interest in magic, the occult and life after death. They may use Tarot cards, or other means of divination, all the while making disparaging remarks about the practice. Often they are deeply and often wordlessly religious. Others may be much more prosaic, but they are still likely to search for some experience beyond the commonplace, even if they do not recognise it as such. For instance an atheistic Nine may deny all belief in anything non-corporeal, yet feel a profound love of nature. Nines are rarely sentimental, and this emotion will be expressed by a liking to be alone in wood and field, sitting quietly by a stream, perhaps fishing or even farming. All this is perfectly ordinary, but a true Nine will be taking in a great deal more than fresh air, even if he or she has not found a name for it. Nines are fundamentally renewed by communing with something larger than themselves.

As we saw, Type One, the New Moons display a dichotomy. While they are excited by future possibilities they feel constrained to bear tradition in mind. A similar combination is found in Nines, but with the emphasis on the past. Nines are not particularly attracted by innovations. They feel 'Plus ça change, plus c'est la même chose.' (It must be noted that if the Moon is very close to New, Nines will be proportionately more enthusiastic about novelty.) None the less they feel the 'presence' of the future in a very real way. Some do literally possess a quality of seership. They are also bone-hard sceptics and will submit any 'experiences' they have to stern questioning. This renders what they do sense all the more valuable.

Nines are not prone to fudge issues. They will not bend over backwards to spare your feelings. Any wounds they may carry from childhood tend to heal only slowly. That is why the picture of them sounds sometimes gloomy. Life can be hard for them. However, the depth that Nines possess can be rich and delicious. Many of them are intensely creative people with much to contribute to family and community. Others seem to have their own private gateway to another world, like the doorway to the magical land of Narnia, found in the wardrobe of *The Lion, the Witch and the Wardrobe*. You are privileged if shown this. There is a depth of kindness and dedication within Nines that is unparalleled once it is accessed. You

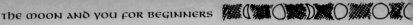

may not pick them out in a crowd, but these people are seldom ordinary.

RELATIONSHIPS

There tends to be an all-or-nothing quality to Nine relationships. Like New Moons, if they decide they have found 'the One' they will put a good deal of emotion and energy into the partnership. Nines can feel they are in love for life, and this can be literally true. Their feelings do not readily change, although they may not express them. Sometimes they conceal them even from themselves, and that is unfortunate. The repressed feelings then carry out guerrilla warfare, as it were, from the shadowlands. It is not good to be ambushed by jealousy during a family breakfast! To make matters worse Nines will often persist in denial, exuding inkiness into the atmosphere like an octopus behind the newspaper. Nines do well to learn to say gently, 'I really can't help wondering if this person who phones you from the office could be a threat to us. I love you very much and I need to talk it through'. No easy matter for many Nines!

When a Type Nine falls in love their intensity is second to none. The drama of the emotion is like a tempest at sea. They will often hide this as best they can even from the object of their affections, while they scheme and manoeuvre to seduce or possess. Conversely they sometimes 'go for broke' with a passionate declaration. Nines give a lot when they give their heart, and to be loved by such a one can be a wild and magical experience.

On the other hand Nines can be cynical about relationships, going through life from one sexual encounter to the next with an arid lustfulness. This puts them in touch with their animal depths if not their emotional ones. Occasionally they will opt for celibacy, taking their 'untouchableness' to the literal extreme. Sometimes they are very inhibited and feel that certain things are forbidden, however much they tell themselves this is not so. But generally they prefer sexual experimentation, either within a stable relationship or a string of casual encounters. Perhaps more than any other Phase they are prone to extreme sexuality and to what is commonly called

perversion. Nines' palates are often jaded – some are that way even as virgins, and their tastes can run even beyond what is acceptable even in our liberal times. There may be a touch of sadism in what turns them on. It must be born in mind, however, that the average Nine will be a most desirable sexual partner. At their best they are intense and exciting and truly sincere.

Nines expect a lot from partners in terms of feeling and commitment, which is fine as they have so much to give themselves. Occasionally, however, they can be prone to count what they give, both emotionally and financially very closely, and to demand almost what amounts to sacrifice from a partner. It's as if they feel they are going to be short-changed and so they evoke this in partners by their own streak of meanness that they cannot perceive. After all, they know they are deeply in love. Nines need to remember that love needs to be displayed and acted upon if their relationships are not to founder.

Also, Nines can be suspicious. An awareness of the entire scale of human vices is in their very bones, and it may be hard for them to believe in innocence. If they answer the phone to be greeted by silence or spot a letter addressed to a partner in an unknown hand, they may explode. On the other hand, keeping silence, they can embark on a grim and sordid trail through pockets and diaries. This will be especially noticeable in a Scorpio Nine. It is written, 'Seek and ye shall find,' and unfortunately something to feed suspicion usually turns up. Nines need to be careful not to drive their partner into the very thing they suspect by punishing behaviour. With a bit of understanding this can be averted. The innate wisdom of Nines reasserts itself, and although they may not precisely laugh at themselves there is the possibility of a wry smile.

Nines will sometimes leave anniversaries and birthdays unmarked, because such things seem superficial. They need to remind themselves that others need visible signs of feeling. Cards and bouquets are symbols that set up a positive feedback to enhance the relationship and enrich them deeply.

The quality of 'seership' that some Nines possess can surface at times of emotional stress. One Type Nine woman, suffering at the

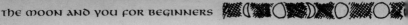

end of a relationship, withdrew to lick her wounds and go early to bed at the end of empty days. She was a level-headed person and an accountant by profession. When she told me that her ex had woken her up one night to tell her he was making love to his new lady I assumed he had phoned her. However, she explained that she had been woken by a sort of electric shock and had heard his voice informing her graphically of what he was up to. 'Just the sort of thing he'd do,' she commented. The following day she swallowed her pride in order to phone him to check out her experience. His stunned silence was all the reply she needed.

Love is a deep matter to Nines, and can be a gateway to hidden places in the personality. Whether that is wonderful or scary depends on your point of view.

FAMILY LIFE

Nines are not always well adapted to family life. They are individualists who may find compromise a strain. As children they can be unreachable and wilful at times. Type Nine children need to be reassured that solitary pursuits are fine if that is what they wish. Their unique ideas need to be listened to by their family, so that they acquire self-respect and the inner strength to weather any incomprehension they may meet elsewhere.

Babies born at this phase of the Moon are especially likely to wear that wise look that speaks of past lives remembered. Type Nine children may be unafraid of things that scare others, but the converse can also be true. Monsters may inhabit the shadows and figures from books and television haunt them by night. These can be helped by strong spiritual or religious guidance. Careful monitoring of what they are exposed to may be necessary. Some will thrive on a diet of horror films that somehow make their inner demons more manageable.

Type Nine parents see in their babies a precious embodiment of life at its most primitive and the promise of a meaningful future. Intensely devoted it may be hard for them to be spontaneous. Often they cannot indulge in play. If life seems to them a serious business

they may come across as harsh and authoritarian in an effort to 'tell it like it is'. This arises from a true wish to do the best for their children, but they may need to remind themselves that the vicissitudes of life are much more readily faced from the basis of a loving and joyful home. Each person must and will face problems in their own way. They cannot prepare children for deprivation by depriving them. None the less, the strength of type Nine parents can be an inspiration. They are always there to name the unnameable and to show that there is a way through even the most thorny problems.

Adolescence is not an easy time. At this age peer pressure can be at its greatest. Most teenagers, although they may rebel fiercely against everything their parents say are complete slaves to the opinions of their contemporaries. For Nines this is a struggle. Some will seek leadership roles, or become very uncommunicative. Mostly they feel misunderstood, and are realising how hard it is for them to 'fit in'. Parents will need to be extremely patient and open-minded. Teenage Nines can be morose or unco-operative. It is important to give them respect and responsibility and to acknowledge that they may know a thing or two, even though they are young. Type Nine parents can be brilliantly understanding of adolescent agonies as long as they are prepared to empathise, not lay down rules.

Step-families can become hell for some Nines and few phases turn more readily into the wicked step-parent. Their partner's past can seem an ever-present shadow and they may feel resentful at not having been part of it. Stepchildren, as a representation of this can become problematic unless efforts are made to achieve a relationship with them as people. If Nines are assured they are respected and listened to, they can adapt. Nines may resent financial outlay on stepchildren and getting maintenance out of an absent Nine parent can be like getting blood out of the proverbial stone.

It is as grandparents that Nines come into their own, and perhaps it is fair to say that many Nines do not realise themselves until they are elderly. They may try to behave as extrovertly as a Type One or Three in order to make their mark on life and to achieve the acceptance that we all crave – even Nines! Type Nine grandparents

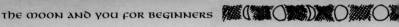

provide a space of calm and total tolerance that is magnetic to young people, where anything they do or think is accepted and sore places healed. Nines of all ages will often actively seek out the aged, enjoying their company and finding fulfilment in caring for them. They see in them the acceptance of life and self which is their own innate gift or goal.

CAREER

Detached though they may be, Nines are often ruthless and determined in their career. In common with the New Moons they have concentration, and feel that 'A thing worth doing is worth doing well.' On occasion they will push themselves in a way that is almost obsessive – they are true 'grafters'. Their drive to get to the top is more a drive to rake the experience of achievement to the limit than the wish for achievement itself. Inside they know that worldly success is empty unless it means something internally, and if this is not consciously realised at first, it is soon arrived at.

We have seen that Nines do not take to half-measures, and some will prefer a life of seclusion, out of the rat-race. Like Eights, some may be literally monks or nuns. It is their tendency to be drawn to the mysterious and the hidden in some form. They are not often suited to group activity, unless given their due as 'wiseman' of the office or the assembly line guru. They prefer to lead in some way or to work alone. Having their own business can be an answer for many Nines.

It is sometimes the case that Nines can't 'find themselves' in their employment, or indeed in anything fulfilling. Their resources may feel unreachable or blocked, and if this is the case they will need counselling or hypnotherapy to bring about a change. Some separate home and work, slaving at the former and becoming complete non-participants in the latter. Others will stay with the same company until 'gold watch' time.

Some Nines are frugal and expect colleagues and family to accompany them in self-denial. They can also exhibit gestures of extreme generosity and may give liberally to charity. Usually they

know what they are doing with their money because they perceive it as energy and power, which Nines like to wield. Its concrete value will feel less attractive, except possibly to a Taurus or Virgo. Nines know that someone is going to hold the reigns, and as they have no intention of being controlled by anyone they would rather be in the driving seat. After all, 'He who pays the piper calls the tune.'

Nines are able to show the rest of us the value of courage and commitment, the hidden meanings behind superficial existence and the spark of the eternal within us. Wise Nines provide a quality of stillness that enables the inadmissible to be accepted and old wounds healed.

MAKING THE BEST OF YOURSELF

Many Nines will turn rather sour at the idea that they could improve on their life. It's not that they think they're perfect (although that is possible!) – it's just that all this positive thinking stuff grates. It seems to them that sweetness, light and crystals can be suspect to the point of nausea. Of course, this can be true, and any Nine who tries to blind her/himself to the grimmer side of reality is walking about with their inner eye blindfolded. Having said that, there really is no harm in attempting to dwell on the bright side sometimes.

So come on now, Nines: grit your teeth and ask yourself where you may be acting or thinking in a way that is destructive to your best interests. What are the important elements in your life? Is it a relationship? How much energy are you expending in analysis, suspicion, holding back 'just in case'? How often do you dwell on your lovers' faults, incompatibilities, inconsistencies? Make an effort to count the good things instead, however simplistic this may seem. Send some flowers, buy a card (even if there's no occasion) walk in with a bottle of wine and a smile. You're not going to miss anything, nor are you going to protect yourself by keeping up a shield.

Maybe it's your career that means most to you at the moment. Are you afraid of being exploited, deceived, short-changed? Well, that happens to all of us. Rest assured, you won't miss any important

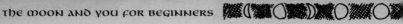

signals by directing your energies into doing the very best you can, and pleasing people where reasonable, even if there is no immediate profit for yourself. Use the quality of 'deep seeing' that you possess to awaken you to the fact that, in the end, one way or another we do get out of life what we put in. Develop a little faith, because it is its own reward, and it lights everything up.

If you are a Nine who feels often depressed, very negative and resentful, with a nose for the compost but never the roses, ask yourself where you have received the message that life is bad, hard and against you. Be ruthless about this. There may be something or someone in your past that you have enshrined in some way, regarding it/them as sacred rather than face the pain of what you haven't had. Examine all your presuppositions. It will help you if you develop the habit of meditating. Sit quietly and comfortably, emptying your mind as thoroughly as you can. Stare at a candle flame, let its stillness pervade you, feel its heat and life in your solar plexus. If you try to be 'positive' you may just irritate yourself, so just absorb the essence of the flame as best you can. Gravitate to anything that gives you peace and stillness, running water, the sea, lakeside or mountaintop. You will need to admit you need healing before you may receive it.

Wisdom is your birthright, but remember it is not only harsh – it is also gentle and serene.

compatibilities

Nines tend to be happy with Eights and sometimes a relationship with a One can be invigorating and can give Nines new perspective. Threes are likely to provoke conflict, and to a lesser extent this can be the case with Sevens. Sixes are also good for Nines. There is often an attraction for Fives although this may be disturbing.

VISUALISATION

Relax yourself, as described in the Introduction.

You are in a cave, deep in the heart of the earth. The atmosphere is peaceful and utterly still. Sweet, secret scents enter your very bones as you breathe in, deeply. You feel warm and completely safe. A dim glow lights your way as you walk along the smooth floor of the cave, towards an underground pool. The surface of the pool is undisturbed except for the occasional gentle ripple that suggests a hidden spring. Its colour is the deepest of greens, with a hint of emerald. There is a faint luminous quality to it. It fills you with wonder. Allow yourself to absorb the peacefulness of the pool for a few moments.

Now as you gaze deeply into the pool you begin to see a tiny point of light, as if the water is reflecting an overhead star. That cannot be, as you are underground, and so the light must come from within the pool itself. It grows and grows until the whole of the pool is filled with scintillating silver light. It glows and shimmers, lighting up the whole cave, banishing the shadows. Now look around you, at what has been revealed by the light. Perhaps there are other cave-dwellers that you can see and speak with, spirits of earth and water with their stories to tell. Perhaps loved ones and friends. Maybe you can see strange subterranean plants or animals, jewels or magical objects. Perhaps you will see nothing, but that doesn't matter. Allow yourself to feel calm and enlivened. Wrap the peace of the cave around you. Feel the energy of the bright pool flowing through your veins. Affirm three times, 'I am peaceful and steady. I love and accept myself and others.'

When you are ready, come back to everyday awareness, bringing with you the feeling of stillness and energy, as if you are a seed waiting for the right time to sprout.

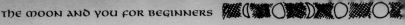

Other Type Nines

Michelangelo, Rimsky-Korsakov, Emily Brontë, Salvador Dali, Bob Dylan, Franz Kafka.

Earthly Harmonies

Colours   Black, deep purple, navy, some deep reds.
Stones   Tourmalated quartz, chalcedony, onyx, obsidian, apache tear.
Herbs, flowers, oils   Myrrh, willow, poppy, pansy, cypress.

12

KEEPING THE
MOON IN MIND

If you have begun to notice the effect of the Moon's phases and have found it interesting, you may like to bring the lunar rhythms more completely into your life. Again, this is not about hedging yourself in, with dos and don'ts – it's about feeling 'alive' and 'in tune'.

If you are a woman you may like to chart your periods with reference to the Moon, seeing how she affects them. If you are a man you could take note of the ups and downs in your physical energy, and record these. Dreams are often influenced by the phase of the Moon, so you may like to jot down some of these. Does your dreamlife increase at the New or Full Moon? Do you dream about different things at different phases?

You could find it a pleasure to celebrate the New or Full Moon in some way – perhaps by buying a bunch of flowers, or opening a bottle of wine. Perhaps you may like to have special pictures or ornaments that you put out at different phases, to keep you 'plugged in'. You only need a small space on a shelf at home to do this. Some lovely cards marking the Moon's phases are available, and so are Moon calendars to chart your month (stockist at the back of the book).

The visualisation exercises given under the 'Types' can be used in any way you like. You may like to use the exercise for your own Type, to enhance your own energies, or you may feel there are other parts of you that are better served by one of the other visualisations. Perhaps you'll just like one better than the others – it's up to you. Also, if you wish, you can do each of them in turn, at the

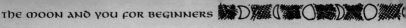

appropriate Moon phase, practising one for three to four days, then turning to the next, and so on, until the cycle is complete. What you are wanting to do is find out some more about yourself, and feel relaxed – that's what it's about.

The character sketches for each of the phases can be read to bring alive the energies current at the time. It is useful to explore our potentials, but we are all aware that we are individuals and cannot be rigidly divided into 'types'. The important message is to find the harmonies for our Phase.

Planning activities by the Moon is nothing new, and gardening is traditionally believed to be especially influenced by the Moon. Here is a chart of the phases and what to do at them:

Phase One (New Moon)

On the first day of the New Moon it's better not to surge into action. Feel a sense of new beginnings, play with ideas, feel excited. Begin action on Day 2. Plant seeds of herbs, flowering annuals and vegetables that grow above ground. Take the first steps in new projects. Now is the time to take the initiative in matters you've been hesitating about. Apply for a job, start a relationship.

Phase Two

Sow lawns, and anything covering a large area. Repot houseplants, reorganise garden (if you wish). Start redecorating the house. Go on holiday. Contact friends, arrange meetings. Increase communication, whether business or personal. Now is the time to get into your stride with your projects.

Phase Three

Pick fruit and vegetables that are to be eaten immediately. A high energy time to tackle tougher tasks. Also notice which projects aren't viable at the moment – put them to one side and concentrate your efforts on what you can achieve. Have your hair cut. Have a manicure.

Phase Four

Time to finalise plans for a party or event. Plant out flowering plants. Plant leeks, onions, peas, tomatoes. Check plants over, water them. Pay special attention to anything creative you are doing. Buy new clothes, wallpaper, carpets. Cook for the freezer. Get married! Start a pregnancy (preferably in that order!)

Phase Five (Full Moon)

Have a party. Go to the theatre, cinema, go for walks. Complete projects as far as possible. Allow your imagination full reign – you never know what might come to light. Work on into the night if you feel inspired. Add fertiliser in the garden, and plant seeds now if the weather has been very dry. This can also be a time for reflection – about goals in life, family, relationships, etc. Intuition can be strong in some people at this time, so if you want to practise the Tarot or other forms of divination, now could be a good time.

Phase Six

Put finishing touches and frills on what you've been doing. Plant carrots, potatoes, radishes, turnips. Plant trees. Listen to music, enjoy paintings, drink in landscapes. If you've had a row with someone, but you don't really feel the issues are important, make up.

Phase Seven

Have a thorough sort-out – throw out rubbish, kill weeds, mow lawns. Think about what you've been doing – are there some things you want to abandon or change? What does it all mean to you? Gather more information on your projects, if you need to. Slow down the activity, perhaps, and step up the thinking.

Phase Eight

Take time for rest. Meditate if you can. Make few demands on yourself. If you feel discouraged this won't last – use the time for playing with ideas. Day-dream if you like, but make sure your

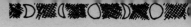

dreams contain a seed of the possible that you can grow when the Moon waxes. Dry herbs and flowers. Harvest produce for storage such as apples and potatoes.

Phase Nine

Give yourself time for seclusion, if that's what you want. Sift, analyse, discard, plan. Make endings, clear spaces (physically and emotionally). Cut wood or prune plants and trees, but other gardening activities are best left. Let creativity take a back seat for a few days, and give yourself a chance to find out what you really want for the future – it may have changed. Don't be afraid to let go. As at Full Moon, now can be a time of 'hunches' but these may tend to relate more to inward matters now. You may suddenly realise how you really feel about something, and decide to act upon it as the Moon waxes.

We have talked about the energy surge at New Moon and the climax of Full Moon. However, each of us has our own special time in the Moon's cycle – that time that coincides with the phase of the Moon when we were born. This is a time of intensity. Specifically Type Ones may feel especially excited, full of new ideas, but also doubts, when the Moon is new. Twos may find they accomplish most and feel at their most positive at their phase. Threes may feel a huge energy surge at their time, and may need to modify this if they feel frustrated and rebellious. Fours are likely to feel at their most ebullient and unstoppable, and Fives, at Full Moon may feel inspired and clear-sighted (or perhaps tired and 'weird'). Sixes are likely to find their time corresponds to feeling especially harmonious and peaceful, enjoying all their projects and if you are a Type Seven you may feel an extra need to explore meanings, find things out and discuss things when the Moon is at your birth phase. Eights may feel especially otherworldly during their phase, and may be advised to take special note of their dreams, while Nines may feel a particular urge for solitude, or at least to 'commune with themselves' in some inner way, at their time. It can be a good idea to be aware when the phase of the Moon corresponds to your birth phase – approximately – for those few days may be valuable to your self-expression.

Finally, remember that it is your inner feelings that count. The whole point of observing the natural rhythms of the Moon is to make contact with your instincts – so follow them in the final instance, not a timetable.

And enjoy the Moon – she's beautiful!

APPENDIX 1 TABLE ONE: FINDING YOUR MOON LETTER

	January	February	March	April	May	June	
A	1, 2, 3	1, 2	1, 2, 3	1, 2	1, 2	1, 2, 3	A
B	4, 5, 6	3, 4, 5	4, 5, 6	3, 4, 5	3, 4, 5	4, 5, 6, 7	B
C	7, 8, 9, 10	6, 7, 8, 9	7, 8, 9	6, 7, 8	6, 7, 8	8, 9, 10	C
D	11, 12, 13	10, 11, 12	10, 11, 12, 13	9, 10, 11, 12	9, 10, 11, 12	11, 12, 13	D
E	14, 15, 16	13, 14, 15	14, 15, 16	13, 14, 15	13, 14, 15	14, 15, 16, 17	E
F	17, 18, 19, 20	16, 17, 18, 19	17, 18, 19	16, 17, 18	16, 17, 18	18, 19, 20	F
G	21, 22, 23	20, 21, 22	20, 21, 22, 23	19, 20, 21, 22	19, 20, 21	21, 22, 23	G
H	24, 25, 26	23, 24, 25	24, 25, 26	23, 24, 25	22, 23, 24, 25	24, 25, 26	H
I	27, 28, 29, 30	26, 27, 28	27, 28, 29	26, 27, 28	26, 27, 28	27, 28, 29	I
A	31	29	30, 31	29, 30	29, 30, 31	30	A
B							B

	July	August	September	October	November	December	
B	1, 2	1, 2, 3, 4	1, 2, 3	1, 2	1	1, 2, 3	B
C	3, 4, 5, 6	5, 6, 7	4, 5, 6	3, 4, 5, 6	2, 3, 4	4, 5, 6, 7	C
D	7, 8, 9	8, 9, 10	7, 8, 9	7, 8, 9	5, 6, 7	8, 9, 10	D
E	10, 11, 12	11, 12, 13, 14	10, 11, 12, 13	10, 11, 12	8, 9, 10, 11	11, 12, 13	E
F	13, 14, 15	15, 16, 17	14, 15, 16	13, 14, 15	12, 13, 14	14, 15, 16, 17	F
G	16, 17, 18, 19	18, 19, 20	17, 18, 19	16, 17, 18, 19	15, 16, 17	18, 19, 20	G
H	20, 21, 22	21, 22, 23, 24	20, 21, 22, 23	20, 21, 22	18, 19, 20, 21	21, 22, 23	H
I	23, 24, 25	25, 26, 27	24, 25, 26	23, 24, 25	22, 23, 24	24, 25, 26, 27	I
A	26, 27, 28	28, 29, 30	27, 28, 29	26, 27, 28	25, 26, 27	28, 29, 30	A
B	29, 30, 31	31	30	29, 30, 31	28, 29, 30	31	B
C							C
D							D

Look up your birthday against the columns of letters on the right and left of the page to find your Moon letter.

N.B. This table is compiled for Greenwich Moon Time. Time in Australia is between 8 and 10 hours ahead of GMT. In the USA

TABLE TWO: FINDING YOUR BIRTH PHASE NUMBER

						A	B	C	D	E	F	G	H	I
1900	1919	1938	1957	1976	1995	1	2	3	4	5	6	7	8	9
1901	1920	1939	1958	1977	1996	4	5	6	7	8	9	1	2	3
1902	1921	1940	1959	1978	1997	7	8	9	1	2	3	4	5	6
1903	1922	1941	1960	1979	1998	2	3	4	5	6	7	8	9	1
1904	1923	1942	1961	1980	1999	4	5	6	7	8	9	1	2	3
1905	1924	1943	1962	1981	2000	8	9	1	2	3	4	5	6	7
1906	1925	1944	1963	1982	*2,000*	2	3	4	5	6	7	8	9	1
1907	1926	1945	1964	1983	*97*	6	7	8	9	1	2	3	4	5
1908	1927	1946	1965	1984		9	1	2	3	4	5	6	7	8
1909	1928	1947	1966	1985		4	5	6	7	8	9	1	2	3
1910	1929	1948	1967	1986		7	8	9	1	2	3	4	5	6
1911	1930	1949	1968	1987		1	2	3	4	5	6	7	8	9
1912	1931	1950	1969	1988		4	5	6	7	8	9	1	2	3
1913	1932	1951	1970	1989		8	9	1	2	3	4	5	6	7
1914	1933	1952	1971	1990		2	3	4	5	6	7	8	9	1
1915	1934	1953	1972	1991		5	6	7	8	9	1	2	3	4
1916	1935	1954	1973	1992		9	1	2	3	4	5	6	7	8
1917	1936	1955	1974	1993		3	4	5	6	7	8	9	1	2
1918	1937	1956	1975	1994		6	7	8	9	1	2	3	4	5

Look up your Moon letter against the year of your birth to find our your birth phase number.

N.B. Many numbers have been crunched into these simple tables. Their accuracy is generally 80 per cent. To be certain of your birth phase you will need an astrologer to draw up your horoscope.

APPENDIX 2 – HOW TO MAKE YOUR MOON OBSERVANCE CALENDAR

You will need a ruler, pencil, a packet of fine-tipped felt tips and several sheets of lined A4 paper – the extra ones are in case of mistakes! You will also need a diary or calendar showing New and Full Moons for the year in question.

Turn the sheet of paper on to its side, so that the long side is at the top. Draw one line in pencil about two-and-a-half centimetres down the page. Above that line, draw the Full Moon in the centre of the page. About six centimetres to the left of the Full Moon draw the waxing crescent – horns pointing to the left. Six centimetres to the right draw the waning crescent – horns pointing to the right. At each of the top corners draw the dark moon – a faint circle, shaded in.

Now draw 13 more lines underneath the top line, about one-and-a-quarter centimetres apart. Your page is now divided into 13 rows of rectangles.

Turn to your calendar/diary. Which comes first in the year, New Moon or Full Moon? If it is the Full Moon, mark the day number *of the Full Moon* (not the month) in the top centre rectangle, just under your picture of the Full Moon. If the New Moon comes first in the year, mark the date of the first *Full Moon*, similarly *on the second line*. The exception to this is when the New Moon is actually on the first of January. In that case, mark your first Full Moon on the *top* rectangle.

Working backwards, to the left, mark in the other dates, until you get to the date of the New Moon. If the New Moon came first in the year you will still be in January (unless it was on Jan 1st). Mark in December's Full Moon, if you wish, in the top centre rectangle, and fill in the dates towards the right, until you get to the final day before New

Moon. Now that part of your calendar is complete and you will have the picture of how the rest of the calendar will shape up.

Continue marking in the Full Moons, underneath each other, working back to New Moon, and forwards to the day prior to New Moon. The edges won't always be even. When you have finished you can mark in the months at the right and/or left edges. You now have a calendar constructed with the Full Moons in a line at the centre of the page, as the 'peak of the month' but you could equally make a similar calendar with the New Moon at the centre.

You will need your coloured felt-tips for your 'moon observance'. Use them to colour-code your feelings etc. Do you feel angry, aggressive, energetic, sexy? Mark those days with a red A, E or S. Use yellow for clear thought, blue for peaceful and relaxed, green for loving/healing, black or grey for fatigue and depression, and so on. Use colours and symbols as you see fit; don't be afraid to use your imagination or your own 'colour-code' – mine is only a suggestion. If you are a woman of menstruating age, frame those days in red (in the case of eclipses, you might like to shade the square grey). If you are a man in close relationship with a woman, you may like to frame *her* menstruating days on your calendar – believe me, they will affect you in more ways than the obvious!

Once you are used to making 'moon observance' you may think of all sorts of variations of your own – for instance you may prefer to plot each month separately, in a circle. Feel free to do whatever appeals. Develop it – and enjoy it!

FURThER READING

The Lunar Almanac, Rosemary Ellen Guiley, Judy Piatkus Publishers, 5 Windmill St, London W1P 1HF, 1991. Full of fascinating lunar lore, and some astronomy.

The Witches' Goddess, Janet and Stewart Farrar, Phoenix Publishing, 1987. Comprehensive and inspiring book about the different forms of the Goddess, through history and from divers cultures.

The Case for Astrology, J. A. West and J. G. Toonder, Penguin, 1973. Many strong arguments supporting astrology in general.

The Lunation Cycle, Dane Rudhyar, Aurora Press. An astrologers' classic by this highly respected author. Non-astrologers may find it somewhat technical.

The Astrology of Self-Discovery, Tracy Marks, CRCS Publications, PO Box 20850, Reno, Nevada 89515, 1985. Helpful and entertaining about Moon Signs, and other astrological subjects.

The Wise Wound, P. Shuttle and P. Redgrove, Harper Collins, 1994. Important thoughts and information on menstruation, with a whole chapter on links with the Moon.

Moon Signs, Sasha Fenton, Aquarian Press, 1987. Tables for readers to find their Moon sign, with interesting and lively interpretations of the Moon through the zodiac.

Astrology for Lovers, Liz Greene, Unwin, 1986. Don't be misled by the title! This is a wickedly accurate, profound and helpful book about the twelve signs, as Sun, Moon and Rising Signs, with a table to find the reader's Rising Sign at birth.

The Sea Priestess, Dion Fortune, Aquarian Press, 1989. A good novel by this well-known occultist – full of Moon lore.

USEFUL ADDRESSES

Faculty of Astrological Studies
BM 7470
London WC1N 3XX, UK. Tel. 0171 700 6479

Information on courses and consultants to draw up and interpret the birth-chart.

W. Foulsham & Co.,
Yeovil Rd,
Slough SL1 4JH, UK.

General astrological and New Age publications, especially planetary tables, to establish position of the planets at birth.

Dark Moon Designs,
20 Bristol Rd,
Brighton BN2 1AP, UK. Tel. 01273 623321

Attractive cards and calendars, good for Moon observance and related themes.

To order this series

All books in this series are available from your local bookshop or, in case of difficulty, can be ordered direct from the publisher. Just fill in the form below. Prices and availability subject to change without notice.

To : Hodder & Stoughton Ltd, Cash Sales Department, Bookpoint, 39 Milton Park, Abingdon, OXON, OX14 4TD, UK. If you have a credit card you may order by telephone – 01235 831700.

Please enclose a cheque or postal order made payable to Bookpoint Ltd to the value of the cover price and allow the following for postage and packing: UK & BFPO: £1.00 for the first book, 50p for the second book and 30p for each additional book ordered up to a maximum charge of £3.00. OVERSEAS & EIRE: £2.00 for the first book, £1.00 for the second book and 50p for each additional book.

Please send me

	copies of	Title	Price	
	0 340 62082 X	Chakras	£5.99	£
	0 340 64804 X	Chinese Horoscopes	£5.99	£
	0 340 60882 X	Dowsing	£5.99	£
	0 340 60150 7	Dream Interpretation	£5.99	£
	0 340 62079 X	Feng-Shui	£5.99	£
	0 340 60883 8	Gems & Crystals	£5.99	£
	0 340 60625 8	Graphology	£5.99	£
	0 340 62080 3	I-Ching	£5.99	£
	0 340 64805 8	Love Signs	£5.99	£
	0 340 64835 X	Meditation	£5.99	£
	0 340 59551 5	Numerology	£5.99	£
	0 340 59552 3	Palmistry	£5.99	£
	0 340 62081 1	Runes	£5.99	£
	0 340 59553 1	Star Signs	£5.99	£
	0 340 59550 7	Tarot	£5.99	£
	0 340 65495 3	Visualisation	£5.99	£
			TOTAL	£

Name ....

Address ....

....

.... Post Code ....

If you would prefer to pay by credit card, please complete:

Please debit my Visa/Access/Diner's Card/American Express (delete as appropriate) card no:

☐☐☐☐☐☐☐☐☐☐☐☐☐☐☐☐☐☐

Signature .... Expiry Date ....

For sales in the following countries please contact:
UNITED STATES: Trafalgar Square (Vermont), Tel: 802 457 1911
CANADA: General Publishing (Ontario), Tel: 445 3333
AUSTRALIA: Hodder & Stoughton (Sydney), Tel: 02 638 5299